P9-CDQ-089

Been There, Done That

Angie Brady

Angie Brady

Tysseland Publications

Copyright ©1997 by Angela Brady

All rights reserved. No part of this book may be reproduced in any manner without written permission from the publisher.

Printed in the United States of America

Published by Tysseland Publications
762 S. Rosemont St.
Mesa, Arizona 85206

First Edition

Edited by Kathy Paulson

ACKNOWLEDGMENTS

My heartfelt thanks to the following:
My parents, Albert and Selma Erickson, whose lives
inspired many of these vignettes.
Marie Saterbak, for motivating me to start writing.
Muriel McGrath, who before her death, prodded
me to publish.
Edith Emmons, my mentor.
Kathy Paulson, for her proficiency in deciphering and
editing my writing.
Bill, my husband, without whose encouragement and
patience this book could not have been published.

DEDICATION

To my husband, Bill Brady

To my sons, Mike, Brad and Dave Jenkins

and their families

In memory of my son, Douglas Eric Jenkins

CONTENTS

OF BOOKS AND FRIENDS

Choosing a friend and choosing a book are similar. A new acquaintance, like a book's opening sentence, may spark my interest. I scan both books and people during first encounters. Unlike books, people scanning is reciprocal, subtle, not awkward.

Books have a formative first chapter before I merge with the writer as the story unfolds; even as my friends evolve from mutual attraction and interests to maturation with its trust and interdependence.

My library is colorful with red, black, blue, green and purple dust jackets. My friends are colorful, too. I keep books and friends until the dust jackets are ragged and the friends' faces, as my own, sag and develop wrinkles. Facelifts reduce wrinkles and books may be rebound. Nonetheless, I appreciate wrinkles with distinctions as well as broken book bindings, well worn and comfortable.

Unlike autobiographies, biographies have a long shelf life. A well-written biography is a delightful quiet read and, although I may have to put it down for a time, if it is a tale of a life well lived, I yearn to return to reading it. A biography reminds me of a thoughtful friend whom I may pattern myself after. That friend who has become as close as a member of my family. I become thoughtful when I read of Abraham Lincoln and his role in American history.

I am thankful when I read of Eleanor Roosevelt's crusade for human rights.

An intense person may become as much a pain in the neck as a long involved historical novel which covers generations. I don't have the time or energy to become involved with either of them.

I adore the classics and reread them. Some have broken bindings and coffee spotted pages, their dust jackets so ragged I have to remove them. They, as old friends, can keep me enthralled for hours—the conversation never dull or boring. When we are out adventuring, we laugh and cry together. As a beloved poem memorized during childhood, they bring me comfort and continuity.

If I were limited to a library of four books, I would choose the King James Bible in large print, a Betty Crocker cookbook resplendent with photographs of food, Markings by Dag Hammarskjold and an anthology of poetry. The anthology would include Whitman, Elliott, Dickinson and for fun and ego, one of my own poems.

I keep a copy of Hammarskjold's Markings in Minnesota and in Arizona. My three favorite quotes from his book are:

"Never look to test the ground before taking your next step: only he who keeps his eye on the far horizons will find the right road."

"On maturity: Among other things not to hide one's strength out of fear and consequently live below one's best."

"You have to be severe with yourself in order to have the right to be gentle with others."

Reference books are housed in my antique library table. I use them often. The dictionary as indispensable as my pastor. I consult Webster for spelling a word and my pastor for living the Word.

Both old and new friends are irreplaceable. My bookcase, as my life, is filled with some of each. I mourn a lost friend and a misplaced book.

My oldest books remain, as my oldest friends, in Minnesota. Each summer brings a catch up visit with them. The newest books and friends in Arizona. Wonderful books, wonderful friends. I would be hard pressed to choose between them.

The last chapter or page of a book is always a mystery. If I read ahead, it spoils the plot, or I can't fathom its meaning. A book, as my life, unfolds gradually.

A FATEFUL BID

My parents met at a basket social, a festive event staged each fall in the "country club" of this rural community—the town hall. This hall, a white frame structure, looked like a rural schoolhouse without its bell tower.

Each lovely lady filled her cardboard box with goodies for two and tucked in a slip of paper with her name, sometimes accompanied by a little rhymed poem. She trimmed her box with ruffles made from crepe paper or pictures of flowers cut from the pages of a seed catalog.

The young men walked around the table appraising the baskets in order to choose which one to bid. Most had a clue for the younger siblings were bribed to describe their sister's box. Candy talked.

Dad joined the line with the rest of the men and fate intervened when he took a fancy to a small shoebox covered in blue.

The auctioneer, a local young man, had the reputation of being the best auctioneer in the county. The room fell quiet but for the brisk bidding.

"What am I bid for this lovely blue basket?"

And the auctioneer held up Mother's box with a smile.

"Two dollars, two dollars, who'll give me three?"

Dad upped to five and the bidding became brisker.

"Five dollars and who'll make it ten?"

"Ten dollars," came a voice from the rear.

Dad, determined, said firmly, "Fifteen."

"Fifteen once—fifteen twice. Sold for fifteen dollars."

Fate smiled on my parents-to-be.

Dad opened the basket to find not only two pieces of chocolate layer cake with fudge frosting, but a slip with his lunch partner's name. He held the box high on his hand until Mother acknowledged her basket.

He noticed Mother's blue challis dress matched the blue of her basket and that her brown hair, cut in a stylish bob, curled on her forehead. Her tiny feet were encased in new pumps which only that morning were removed from that small shoebox.

Having come to the social with two of her sisters, she readily accepted Dad's offer to take her home. She had admired the trim stranger as he entered the room.

He took her small hand, helping her over the running board of his Model-T Ford. The two talked of many things during the three-mile drive to her home. Mother knew his fine Norwegian farm family for just the year before she had played opposite his brother in a one-act comedy It's All A Mistake—the mistake being the heroine married the wrong brother.

Soon they became steadies and three years later they married.

Dad insisted it was the chocolate cake with the thick fudge frosting that won his heart.

Notwithstanding the cake, I'm delighted my parents met at the basket social for I can't imagine my life without them.

GOALS

I set a goal when I was five
to dress my paper dolls by noon.
Making paper doll dresses
from Chrismas card envelope liners
of mother of pearl,
of sheer tissues of red, green or blue
or any imaginable hue.
Now I'm an adult,
more than fifty,
wondering what to do with my life,
what goal to set by noon,
same as when I was five.

THE LITTLE GRANARY THAT WAS

Our granary was an eyesore, its red paint peeling from an undercoat of blue, exposing large areas of rain-thirsty timber to the duststorms of the thirties.

A seven-rung ladder nailed to the wall of one of the two small grainbins provided access to a storage area. A wonderful place for me to explore.

My kittens, one orange named Tabby, the other two named Midnight and Star, enjoyed exploring as much as I. They grew fat feasting on field mice who had grown fat feasting on grain.

Three cardboard boxes were stored under the low rafters. I spent happy hours rummaging through them—silent hours shattered by an occasional squeal when a kitty, successful in her grisly hunt, captured a mouse.

One box, smaller than the others, contained letters Dad received during World War I, serving in France. My curious eyes were disappointed for the mice had shredded them so finely the writing was nonrecognizable.

However, the browntone photographs were undamaged. There were more than a dozen pictures of young men in khaki—somber-faced young men with short hair and no sideburns. All looked alike except for my father whom I considered to be the most handsome.

The women, dressed in lace-trimmed white blouses, were lovely. One, photographed in profile, hair high above her forehead, looked as beautiful as my Mother. She resembled the cameo broach mother wore, deep on her bosom. I, a romantic child, knew she was my father's first love.

Dad's helmet was the crown jewel of the war memorabilia. Made of steel, I pictured it heavy on his head, protecting him from a fatal bullet. It surprised me to learn he also used it for bathwater.

The aluminum mess kit resembled my dog Patsey's dish. Each Christmas Dad told of a much anticipated Christmas goose dinner when he received the tip of the wing in his mess kit. Never did I see my father eat a wing.

Deep in the box, I discovered a burlap sack tied with a kahki shoelace which contained a stash of European coins. I spent hours admiring the faces of the kings and queens as I counted and stacked the coins into high piles. One small silver coin, worn smooth from its use, was my favorite. Later, after Dad gifted me the money, I stored this coin in a tiny blue velvet bag.

Both bins were full of grain after the fall threshing. One day, I sank up to my neck in the wheat while wading to the ladder. Terrified as the grain closed around me, I started to scream. Patsey, standing in the doorway, barked until Dad came and rescued me. I never walked through the grain again. Not as much for fear of suffocation but for fear of another spanking.

The little red granary became obsolete, replaced by a steel grain bin. But my memories endure. I wish I had kept Dad's steel helmet and the picture of his first love.

A SUMMER TREASURE

I lie in my mental hammock dreaming of spring and of returning to my cottage on the bank of a lake which is shaped like a pelican.

My cottage is built of wood and stone but its spirit is built of intangibles. Once it belonged to my aunt and uncle and their spirit endures.

In the eye of my mind, I walk the wooden deck, turn my key in the lock, and enter the kitchen. This same kitchen where my aunt baked hundreds of rolls and dozens of cookies for family and friends. This same kitchen where I knead oatmeal bread and bake an occasional apple pie.

In my imagination I walk into the living room, the heart of the cottage, and curl onto a narrow bench by the fireplace. A fireplace built from the same handsplit field-stone as the church where the family worshipped. A fireplace built to last the century. A fireplace perfect for marshmallow roasts on long summer evenings.

My senses come alive in this place for I can hear my uncle singing great hymns and Norwegian folk songs in his clear tenor voice. I can hear my five cousins singing accompanied by my aunt at the antique organ. Then peace covers me as a warm blanket on a cold day.

Later, I look over the windowbox with its red and purple petunias to see water splashing onto the beach. I remember the hours my cousin and I spent building castles in the sands of Pelican Lake.

I remember family picnics at this cottage. Each family brought not only their voracious appetites but also a dish to serve. Each year the same family jokes and tales were shared. Simple stories. Treats for the soul.

I remember fishing with Uncle Carl in the same aluminum boat which is lying face down on the snowy beach this winter. Indestructible. The same five horse-power motor is stashed on a shelf, its faded paint making its name unrecognizable. A product of the thirties, the motor works well. When we fished with my uncle, the fish clamored to be caught. Always ready, willing and able to take our hook. He sang as he fished. Perhaps fish enjoy tenors, too.

My five cousins and our families share reminiscences freely as we summer on Pelican Lake. Encouraged by the unconditional love of our parents, we continue to enjoy the family dinners complete with the family stories and the tired, old family jokes as we share them freely with our children and our children's children.

Inspired, I dream of carrying my lapdesk and pencil to the blue canvas chair on the beach. My only distractions, a curious chipmunk, peering at me from under a rock, and the great blue heron, knee-deep in water, looking for fish.

Sixty years have passed since this little cottage was built. New carpet, drapes, and fresh paint give it a lift. A bookcase is built to my specifications and stores my favorite books and photographs.

Sheltered by the past, I am free to create new memories from the present. For each summer holds its own treasure. Soon my dreams will materialize and I'll return to another four months in the cottage. My mental hammock, no longer needed, will be folded and placed on the long winter's shelf.

PLAGUES OF THE LAKES

Thousands of us live on the Minnesota beaches each summer. We look forward to a summer haven but backward on the plagues of the lakes.

Dandelions love life at the lakes too, their sunny blossoms turn to delicate but deadly seeds which impregnate the grass around them. Children bring bright yellow bouquets for their mothers until they, too, are taught to hate the dandelions.

We barely outwit the dandelions when the mosquitoes hatch around us. If the lakes are Paul Bunyan's footsteps, the sloughs are his fingerprints, ideal breeding grounds for mosquitoes. We swat the deadly pests and leave bloody stains on our arms or legs. We shudder at the sight of our own blood.

The mosquitoes are brought under control by aerial spraying. Next, the state of lake bliss comes under attack by the gnats. A deadly attack under our glasses and in our ears. Nearly invisible, they hang in clouds and as suddenly as they have appeared, they leave.

The mosquitoes survive a second aerial spraying.

Colonies of fishflies appear. These miniature airplanes squish sticky on our windshields. Like the gnats, they move on quickly.

The mosquitoes survive a third aerial spraying.

Later grasshoppers, as biblical locusts, feed on nearby fields of ripening grain. They, as a mighty army, leave devastation behind.

Fall frost finally finishes off the mosquitoes.

MUCH ADO ABOUT WASTEBASKETS

You can tell alot about people from their wastebaskets. Some baskets, like their owners, are more for show and less for function. Made of brass or copper, they make a statement in a room. But a metallic basket gongs as a noisy cymbal when anything heavier than a tissue is dropped into it.

However, most wastebaskets are lightweight plastic. Cream colored. Utilitarian. As clean as its two-shower-a-day owner.

Yet it is what lies within a basket which defines its owner. A paper profile. From personal letters to bills. From an empty cigarette package to a full one.

Writers throw away mountains of paper, ranging from yellow legal sheets to sophisticated computer paper. This crumpled paper, as a giant yogurt swirl cone, overflows their wastebaskets.

Compulsive folks fold paper into little wads, precise little wads which demonstrate a lack of trust. One would be hard put upon to unfold those tight wads to discover the secret messages.

Angry people tear paper into long strips. These paper knives extend dangerously over the top of their wastebaskets.

We hear about employees high in government circles shredding documents, fine as a carrot fresh from the food processor.

Busy offices use paper shredders, too. Some of the

shredded materials in both government and business are more colorful than a carrot and not as life affirming.

Well-organized types remind themselves of just about everything. Their wastebaskets are full of little yellow 2 x 2 squares of paper. Evidently most super-organized folks are not fearful of wastebasket entry and search.

All this much ado about wastebaskets reminds me of my new white wicker wastebasket which needs emptying.

LIFE ON A BIKE

"Turn the way you fall," Dad shouted as he ran behind me on my first bicycle ride. I turned the way I was falling and fell. In a few days, I could control my new Sears bike. Its name was Elgin, its color blue. A gift for my twelfth birthday, it was the delight of my life.

Soon after, my nine-month-old sister, Marie, and I went for a ride to visit the neighbors. She sat confidently in my bicycle basket and smiled while holding my left hand, my right hand on the handlebars.

We were nearly at their driveway when the wheel skidded in the gravel. I felt that same skidding in my chest. Her small hand in mine, I walked the bike up the driveway and after a short visit, all the way home. I was one scared twelve-year-old.

For my fortieth birthday, my family gave me a lavender Schwin. A beauty with plump white sidewalls. It still, as an aging woman whose wrinkles don't show, looks good from a distance.

Biking has always been a delight as well as transportation for me. In the fifties, I was called the "biking nurse." Now that biking is popular with all ages, I fancy myself a pace setter. Although my legs are older and less muscular, the joy of biking endures. Those two wheels give me a feeling of power—as if I am going someplace. Fast.

Now I travel a mere fifteen blocks, whereas once I wheeled fifteen miles. Now I pedal the paved streets of a retirement community. Once I travelled the gravel roads, an occasional rut upsetting my balance. I fantasize riding a red bike, honking my heavenly horn at the age of 100.

FRONT PORCH MEMORIES

Each summer we moved. Not far. Only to the front porch. Our house, with its three tiny rooms topped by an attic, had no cross-ventilation and became as a sweat shop in the summers so that the porch, larger than our living room, was a healthy escape from the heat. But not from the dust. For the thirties were hot and dry years during which the dust moved freely. Mother kept the furniture dust free with a damp cloth and mopped the green concrete floor daily.

The porch was a splendid center for all our summer activities. Mother cooked on the wood range in the tiny kitchen and I carried the dishes to the white porcelain table on the porch.

She entertained friends and neighbors, serving homemade root beer poured with white froth into thin green goblets, accompanied by a plateful of datebars or frosted ginger cookies topped by coconut. Sometimes both. Mother, a master baker, frequently won blue ribbons at the Clay County Fair.

A tall, white rocker with a flowered blue chintz cushion stood in the far corner of the porch. Mother rocked often. The midday double digit heat was oppressive and she fanned her pink face with a folded newspaper.

The blue terrycloth daybed, borrowed from the living room for the summer, became my bed. Its steel springs snapped my back when I changed position. If my cousin spent the night, the cot was opened to a double bed. The springs, like a hammock, tossed us toward its center.

In the evenings we lowered the orange and green awnings. This created a cozy privacy. The awnings also kept out the infrequent rain. On stormy nights when the wind blew the rain under the awnings, I carried my wet pillow and sheets into the living room and made a bed on the floor.

We played games on cool porch evenings. There were no cards in our home. Only a faceless card game. Dad won. Always.

We stored the checker board and marbles in a box under the daybed. It was mother's favorite game because she won. I knew it was because she insisted on using the blue marbles and I was relegated to using the amber ones.

Patsey, my faithful collie, enjoyed the move to the porch as much as the rest of the family. After her plateful of table scraps, she lay content under the table.

My parents taught me directions from that front porch. If I faced the porch door, I was looking north. My right hand, east, and my left hand, west. Having no innate sense of direction, I to this day, imagine myself in that porch in order to tell directions. This takes time.

And I have to but close my eyes to feel the cool spring breezes on the front porch of my childhood home.

If the breeze is from the north, I can smell the lilacs by the front door.

SPRING WELCOME

Chattering birds interrupt my sleep
this first day at the beach.
I tiptoe from my bed
to see a fading moon.
The mist rises from the lake
and cocoons my soul.
A heron, great and blue,
searches for unwary fish.
Pink petunias in my windowbox
offer a hummingbird a drink.
Smells and sounds of spring
blossom in my nose and ear
and inspire my languid self
as I am welcomed home.

NO EARTHLY REASON

The telephone rings with an unexpected urgency.
"Hello."

I hear sobbing.

"Angie, it's Alicia. Will you come to the hospital? I'm having surgery tomorrow - heart surgery."

It is the mid-sixties and heart surgery is new in this midwestern city. I hurry to the hospital. Alicia shows me three watercolors.

"I just finished this one last night, Angie."

It is a lovely painting of pink and blue wildflowers with mountains in the background.

"One painting for each of my children. I want them to have something to remember them by."

"Remember you by?"

Chilled, I sit and listen.

She talks of her estrangement from her son Jim. Long-haired and idealistic, Jim left home after a fight over that long hair.

"I don't know where he is, Angie. Maybe I'll never see him again."

Making an effort to control her sobbing, she talks of her approaching surgery.

"I'll die, Angie, and they'll say, 'We don't know what went wrong.'"

I leave the hospital preoccupied with our conversation, miss the turn toward home and take an alternate route. Crossing the bridge over the river, I see a familiar long-haired, jean-clad boy walking on the sidewalk.

"Jim, I'm so glad to see you. Get in the car. Jim, your mother is in the hospital - she is having heart surgery in the morning. She really wants to see you. Jim, your mother is dying."

"She'll never accept me, Angie. It's my hair."

"Jim," my voice lowers, "The hair must go."

We drive to the nearest barber shop, The receptionist is locking the door.

"Sorry, it's 5:30. All the barbers have gone home."

"Do you have a wig? A man's wig?"

I hear the urgency in my voice.

Jim's long dark hair bundles easily under the color matched wig. I think how handsome he is, how like his mother's are his features.

Minutes later I drop him at the hospital to visit her.

I am told they had a glorious reunion. A forgiving time. With laughter and tears they recalled the events of the past as they shared the present.

Alicia's surgery, as scheduled, was at eight in the morning.

Pleased, the surgeon reported to the family, "Everything went well."

The family was relieved but kept a vigil throughout the day.

At eight that evening, Alicia's 42-year-old heart stopped.

"We don't know what went wrong," the surgeon said.

Jim gave the eulogy for the family at the memorial service.

I overheard Josie's neighbor, "He looks so handsome—and he even cut his hair."

Some may think it is a coincidence that I found Jim.

GRAPE JELLY

My standard instruction to the waitress is, "No grape jelly, any other kind is fine."

I loathe grape jelly. Anytime, anyplace.

With no discretionary income and four hungry boys, grape jelly was affordable. The bigger the container, the better. A two-pound tin of grape jelly was cheaper than several six-ounce glasses. Except I couldn't reuse the tin.

My sons slathered it on homemade wheat bread. Sometimes they slathered it on pancakes. Or they combined it with peanut butter for a special after-school treat.

The jelly left purple rings around their mouths and stains on their shirts. But it was cheap. Affordable.

Many things were unaffordable; therefore, one of their small pleasures was grape jelly.

THE PSYCHOLOGY OF TRUST

The wheat stood tall, burnished gold, against the horizon on this hot and humid August afternoon. I, Dad's hired hand, was driving the tractor in harvest.

I turned a corner too fast and Dad flew off the mower, missing the razor sharp sickle by inches.

Horrified at what could have happened, I said, "Dad, I'm so sorry."

"It can happen to anyone—don't worry about it," he said as he returned unhurt to his seat.

Later, after we finished mowing the field, he asked, "Angela, will you take the car home? Drive it just like you drive the tractor."

This, even in the forties, was a short driver's training course. With a thumping heart and sweating palms, I drove the Ford V-8 home.

The next day, Dad said, "Now that you are sixteen, we'll go into Sommer's Drug and get you a driver's license."

It was to be years later before I was to recognize that my father knew the psychology of trust.

DAD'S WINDMILLS

Windmills are an artist's delight. They paint them against a red orange sky with blue misty mountains in the background. They paint them standing lonely over long prairie grasses. They paint them catching a glint of sun on their fantail wedges.

Authors depict the windmill in terms of great beauty and romance, signifying the taming of the prairie by ranchers and farmers.

Dad decided to build a windmill for its practical value rather than its asethetic appeal. In our home there was no discretionary income and the wind was free power, therefore practical in the Great Depression.

I pictured his windmill looking like Uncle Ole's windmill, stretching high into the sky on thin but sturdy horizontal and vertical steel beams.

However, he split two large steel barrels and painted them aluminum before attaching them to four long wooden arms. This octopus-like creature was attached to an intricate system of belts and pullies.

His was not a run-of-the-mill windmill. No artist's delight. But he was thrilled to see it catch the wind and pump water for us and the livestock.

Not so my mother. To her, the windmill was an eyesore. A pain to look upon—only fifty feet from her kitchen window. Worse yet, it attracted unwelcome attention for curious passersby stopped their cars to gawk at the strange structure.

Some folks stopped to ask my father how to construct it because they, too, needed free power to pump water. Dad was happy to invite them into our home and they spent hours at the kitchen table, Dad making detailed drawings of his invention. For free.

Mother didn't make coffee or even lemonade to serve her uninvited guests. The windmill became as a chill wind from the north in their marriage.

In time, nature intervened and the aluminum paint peeled, leaving the barrels rusty. Therefore, the ugly windmill became uglier.

Mother brought her full power of persuasion upon my father and the monstrosity was replaced by a noisy gasoline engine. Again marital harmony prevailed in our household.

But Dad was restless and needed another project. He read far into the winter nights about windmills generating electric power and soon he built a second windmill—one of which Mother approved.

He devised a windcharger and mounted it on top of our house. Its undernourished wooden arms caught the wind and charged the six batteries located in the far corner of my attic bedroom.

Dad wired our house for electricity. If it was windy, we had bright lights. If not, the lights grew dim and flickered. We used kerosene lamps as a backup. This electricity didn't work on appliances so we continued to use the gas stove and make our toast in the oven.

Although Dad was an avid photographer, developing pictures in his darkroom, no pictures exist of either windmill. I've searched through boxes of old photographs and concluded there are none. Not strange. I expect Mother didn't encourage the pictures of the strange tin monster which blew a cold wind on her marriage.

My memories of those aluminum arms catching the breezes and pumping forth water are as vivid as any photograph.

FENCE TALK

Fences are as diverse as people. They come in all shapes and sizes. They fence people out and fence people in and sometimes it's hard to tell the difference.

From my kitchen window I see a brick wall with brickwork forming an intricate pattern. It creates a barrier between my friendly neighbor and myself. A barrier called a fence.

It is different from the first fence I can remember. That fence, made of wire with sharp wire thorns, was sharp enough to catch and tear my clothing and scratch my legs when I climbed over it.

These wire thorns kept our cows in their pasture, away from the gravel road with cars speeding forty miles an hour. Even forty-five.

When the fence broke, the cows bolted into new found freedom. Automobile brakes squeaked as the cows crossed the road looking for a greener pasture.

Classic white picket fences require frequent repainting to retain their storybook appearance. But ranch type wood fences are easy care. This wood, as people, becomes more beautiful with age. Weathered.

All fences are enhanced by flowers which make them more people friendly. I prefer sunflowers.

MORE THAN YOU WANTED TO KNOW
ABOUT OUTHOUSES

A bit of Americana vanished with the demise of the outdoor toilet. These small square buildings were the butt of dozens of cartoons and jokes. Pranksters created chaos by tipping them every Halloween.

The two-holer on our farm was located at the end of a long dirt path. It was hidden discreetly behind the granary.

Why a two-holer, I don't know, for I never saw anyone use the second hole. Perhaps it was an emergency hole. Just in case.

This toilet had a high shelf which Dad rigged for summer showers. It was a sturdy shelf. Sturdy enough to hold a tall pail of warm water with a hose and sprinkler. After siphoning a few mouthsful, I had a stream and voila—a shower!

Toilet paper was an unheard of luxury. Sears and Montgomery Ward catalogues from the previous season worked well, except for the glossy sections. But peach wrappers were a delight. My grandmother ironed every wrapper and cut them in two. She was one economical lady.

Someday I hope to find scented peach toilet paper on the supermarket shelves.

HAPPINESS

Happiness is a fragile state of being,
temporary, as a shimmering bubble
which dissolves with reality
and vanishes to nothingness.
Yet it sparks another fantasy
finding a lively awareness
and in its wake, hope.

THE OLD SETTLER'S PICNIC

Viking Park, near Rollag, Minnesota, was the site of the Old Settler's Picnic on a June Sunday each summer. The five Lutheran congregations in Pastor S.G. Hauge's parish were represented. It was well attended from ten in the morning until five in the afternoon. Families, from babies to grandparents, flocked to this yearly event. Most years the day was sunny but rain was welcome to the farmers and the picnic was postponed a week. If it showered during the day, we took refuge in cars until the showers passed over.

This park had several buildings, a cook kitchen, concession stand and an enclosed speakers' platform. This platform was large enough to hold the combined choirs of all five churches.

In front of the speakers' platform, planks placed on tree stumps provided seating with unlimited standing room. Services were at 11 a.m. A pump organ was loaned from Rollag Church and hymnbooks were provided from the other churches.

Music was abundant for each church had a female as well as a male soloist. A male or female quartette and a duet sung by two sisters were popular. Often a child would solo.

I enjoyed the singing, but not the preaching, because many sermons were in Norwegian in honor of the old settlers who emigrated from Norway. I noted tears on the faces of the elderly women as Pastor Hauge recalled their land of fjords and trolls. They wiped their eyes under their gold-rimmed glasses with handkerchiefs embroidered in all four corners with roses or daisies.

One by one these old settlers died. A memorial for each was included in the next year's sermon.

The afternoon program was more informal and in English. There were more solos, duets and quartettes. Many of the speakers were politicians, incumbents and those aspiring to office. Both local and state, Democrat and Republican. Friendly men in blue serge suits, their knees baggy and seats shiny from sitting at too many harvest home country church chicken dinners. Their shoes, well-polished, had worn soles from making the rounds of picnics such as these. "Stumping."

These speeches seemed long and exceeded my attention span. Therefore, I walked between the plank seating and the concession stand. Sometimes one speaker lasted throughout two bottles of grape pop.

Afterward, the politicians worked the park. They pressed the flesh and kissed the babies. They inquired about the crops and bemoaned the Depression but rarely became involved in controversial issues.

To a youngster like me, it was a time to dress in my summer best dress. One year, a yellow organdy with three tiers of ruffles. Mother had curled my hair in rags so I had "sausage" curls.

I joined my clique of Erickson girl cousins who were also wearing their summer Sunday best. We talked little girl talk, which even at that age, centered on boys. Those same boys who were roaming the grounds with their boy clique.

Soon the cliques joined to play Farmer in the Dell and Drop the Hankie. The love of my life, who didn't know it, was there too. But by this time, my corkscrew brown curly hair was drooping, my new yellow organdy dress had a three corner tear and my white shoes were blackened by dust. My girl cousins, however, still looked fresh and neat.

Many romances had their beginnings and flourished in Viking Park. Young men and women met and visited. The young man made a date for the movies or for next Sunday's Luther League. Luther Leagues were attended with a full church of all ages.

The next summer these couples attended the Old Settler's Picnic. Many times the third finger on the girl's left hand sported a diamond.

The second year they came as a married couple and by the third year they returned as parents of a beautiful baby. For all Rollag babies were beautiful and smart.

My mother and her friends, second generation Norwegians, were the designated workers. They cooked coffee on the kerosene stove in the cook kitchen where it was not unusual to be over a hundred degrees.

The women organized this giant potluck on a long table adjacent to the shanty door. The flies were as abundant as the food.

There were beans of every description, undercooked, hard beans; overcooked soft beans; light beans and dark molasses beans. No two bean pots were alike. Gelatin salads reigned as queens of the table. Red, orange and yellow gelatin, with or without bananas; some with whipped cream and walnuts.

There were scalloped potatoes and macaroni and tomato hotdish with meatballs. There were potato salads decorated with little rounds of hard-boiled eggs. Some of the egg yolks were sprinkled with paprika. The salad bowls were rimmed by garden leaf lettuce.

Sandwiches were of potted meat, egg salad, dried beef and peanut butter, some on homemade white buns. Cakes came in all sizes and colors. Chocolate, white spice and angel food were all made from stratch. Prizewinners.

In all this food, I accomplished the impossible. I

found my mother's food for I knew it looked the best. My cousins chose their mother's food, too.

We sat on blankets on the grass with our families. Dad always complained whenever he sat on a blanket to eat food. He said he always wanted his legs under the table—preferably his own table. Women and little girls, all in dresses, sat as ladies with their knees and ankles together.

This gigantic potluck didn't prevent my cousins and me from going to the concession stand within an hour after we had eaten. The ice cream, always vanilla, was scooped by my oldest boy cousin. He looked neat and clean in his white shirt, its long sleeves carefully folded high on his forearm. He smiled as he gave us a generous scoop of ice cream.

After sharing an early supper of plentiful leftovers, as well as a blessing from Pastor Hauge, sunset found us at home in time for the evening chores.

Monday, volunteers stacked the planks from the outdoor arena under the cover of the speaker's stand. The next summer these same volunteers cleaned the building and grounds for the next Old Settler's Picnic.

The original old settlers passed on over the years so the impetus to continue the festival was over.

Now I, the age of those old settlers, see in my mind's eye my mother chatting with her friends at the picnic. They are lovely in their cotton print and voile dresses, their bobbed hair floating in the summer breezes.

BANK NIGHT

A monthly Bank Night was held at Barnesville's Bejou Theater during the forties. The winning ticket was plucked from a large bowl after the movie.

Even "B" movies were well attended for the excitement of the draw drew a large crowd.

I was restless on a cold February evening and wanted to "see a show." My friends had excuses not to go with me.

"Too cold."

"Poor show. Why on earth do you want to see that?"

"Sorry, I have to study."

I walked the six blocks to the theater and, for the first and so far the last time in my life, attended a movie alone.

She was right, I thought, *it is cold. I knew I should have stayed home and studied.* Furthermore, the movie was so boring, I fell asleep.

I awakened with a start when I heard my name over the loudspeaker.

I walked to the front of the theater, climbed the stairs to the stage to receive a check for one hundred dollars. It was a hitherto unknown sum to me and my first check. I was elated.

Patriotic, I bought a fifty dollar war bond.

Then I went shopping. I bought a lovely black dress with two rhinestone trimmed lace pockets on its bodice. I also bought black patent platform pumps.

I had spending money. Enough to treat my friends and myself to ice cream sundaes at the ice cream shop we called "The Old Maids."

GRAND CANYON CAPTURED

We took pictures of the
Grand Canyon
same day, same hour.
Yours, wide angle.
Mine, zoom.
Yours awe inspiring in scope,
mine detail each twig, each rock.
Both capture nuances of color,
purple, pink, red and gold,
with all the hues between
as seen through different lenses.
By your eyes and mine.

NINE WAYS TO REINVENT YOURSELF

I challenge you to self-renewal. No matter your age, no matter how rich or how poor. Reinvent yourself and get more out of life. For each of you has more talent and creativity than you can imagine.

1. Listen to yourself.

And then crept, a little noiseless noise among the leaves, born of the very sigh that silence heaves.

John Keats

Take time to be alone, turn off the radio and television and learn to browse within yourself. Remember previous years. What you enjoyed earlier may lead you to your own special talent.

Ask yourself if you like working alone or with others. Ask yourself if you enjoy working with your hands or if you prefer reading, writing or public speaking.

2. Believe in yourself.

The reason why worry kills more people than work is that more people worry than work.

Robert Frost

Many of us remember the bad and forget the good about ourselves. It takes energy to worry about past mistakes and it takes energy to worry about the future. It takes as much energy to hide your talent.

Channel this energy into new patterns of behavior.

3. Work to believe in your gifts.

Every man has to seek in his own way to make his own self more noble and to realize his own true worth.

Albert Schweitzer

If you are a good reader, practice in front of a mirror for self-confidence. Read into a tape recorder to hear the rhythm of your speech. Read to children. Offer to become a church lector. You can meet like-minded people if you join poetry or play reading groups.

Do you enjoy photography? My friend has become a roving photographer at weddings and anniversaries. Recently she uncovered another new talent. She draws portraits.

Another friend shares her gift of hospitality. Her dinner invitations are coveted. New and old friends gather often around her table.

Persist in adopting a "can do" attitude.

4. Forget worrying about what others may think.
How I like to be liked and what I do to be liked.
Charles Lamb

If friends appear critical of your new activities, invite them to join you. Their lives may change, too!

For years I kept my writing a secret for fear of what others may think or say. I hid my poetry and essays under the lingerie in my drawer. Attending a writers' conference and later joining a writers' group enabled me to acknowledge my writing.

5. Do the thing you are afraid to do.
The only thing I am afraid of is fear.
Bacon

If you yearn to fly in a hot air balloon but have fears, try it. You may enjoy the feeling of weightlessness.

Single? Ask an eligible man to your next party. A friend has been married more than a dozen years to a man she invited to her New Year's party.

6. Visualize success.
The mind is an iceberg. It floats with only one-seventh of its bulk above water.
Sigmund Freud

In the eye of your mind, learn to see yourself succeeding instead of failing. Program yourself for success by visualization.

Visualize yourself speaking with confidence at your high school reunion. Your classmates will see you as competent as you saw yourself prior to your speech.

Visualize your photographs hanging in an art gallery. Aim for it.

Visualize a beautiful flower garden. Then plant and water to make the vision come true.

Visualize your poetry published. Think with your pencil. Your dream may become a reality.

7. Make appointments to be where your talent is in demand.

To find out what one is fitted to do and to secure an opportunity to do it is the key to happiness.

John Dewey

If you enjoy public speaking, join Toastmasters. If you sing, join a choir. If you are gifted at cards, join a card club.

Interested in politics? Become involved with your local precinct. Later you may aspire to join state and national groups.

Consider an adult education or college course.

Create your own opportunities to burnish your talent.

8. Risk

Take calculated risks. That is quite different from being rash.　　　　　*George Patton*

Build on the success you had when you did the things you were afraid to do. Soon the word "risk" will no longer terrify you.

Aim for a newfound talent every three years. You don't have to become an expert. Risk for success.

9. Volunteer

There are two ways of spreading the light. To be the candle or the mirror that reflects it.

Edith Wharton

Volunteer at a hospital. Feed the homeless. Help children with special needs or read to theblind. The list of ways to help others is endless.

Help your brother's boat across the water and your own will reach the shore.

Hindu proverb

Stories abound how full-time employment has come from volunteer work.

Great public rewards go to only a few but improving ourselves is open to each of us. By next year you should be well on the road to reinventing yourself if you take that first step.

AUTUMN FAREWELL

A tinge of autumn fills the air
as I arise and walk the dock,
the lapping of the waves
the only sound on shore.
Suddenly honking fills the air.
Geese in lopsided formation;
they, as I, honking farewell,
flying to a warmer clime.

CALL IT GOURMET

To me, macaroni and cheese has always been an entree of last resort. Resorted to when the grocery money was short or absent.

Because it was a sticky mass of colorless mush, I created a new variation. A macaroni in cream cheese with lumps of cheese, barely melted. It gave the dish a gourmet appearance which made it almost palatable.

Each of my four sons ate at least three helpings of this gourmet delight. So did my husband.

In truth, I have never met a man who didn't consider macaroni and cheese a favorite food. My husband even enjoys the semi-artificial box variety or the frozen variation.

Potato soup was to my mother what macaroni and cheese was to me. For there was little money during the Great Depression. Made of milk, thickened with mashed potato and topped with onion, it was wonderful.

When I see potato soup, I think of home and love—the same way the men in my family think of macaroni and cheese.

A TIME TO PLANT

It is a perfect day for planting flowers, sunny and warm. It is February in Maricopa County, Arizona. A Minnesota transplant, I think how impossible it would be to plant flowers in the cold earth under a mantle of snow.

In high good humor, I drive to the nursery where I am welcomed by the pansies who look at me with round and friendly faces. I find petunias in every shade of red, blue, pink and purple. They remind me of Minnesota.

I luck out with a 30 percent discount and pick seventeen sturdy, yet elegant, purple petunias. I wonder if it is as true when I am old I shall plant purple as it is when I am old I shall wear purple.

I tell the clerk, "I hear the the white flies don't like the color purple."

She says, "I've never heard that before."

I think, *Of course not, I just made it up.*

At home I put on my canvas gloves and dig seventeen holes about 4 x 4 inches with a little garden spade. Then I slip each plant from its plastic prison and place it in the earth. The dark planting soil contrasts with the red soil of the desert. A little fertilizer, a drink of water and all is done. Until I remember those pansy faces and imagine how friendly they'll look under my kitchen window.

SURPRISES

"Come in the bedroom, I have something to tell you."Clint recognized the urgency in Stacy's voice which was low to avoid awakening the sleeping baby.

Stacy was lying on the bed in her slip when he came in. He thought how beautiful she looked, even childlike with her short blonde hair and darkly fringed blue eyes - to say nothing of that figure which had attracted him from the day they met.

"What is it, honey?" He leaned over and patted her gently on the curve of her hip.

"Clint, I just came from Dr. Swanson's office. I'm pregnant."

Stunned, he wondered if he would be able to speak he felt so excited and scared. Through a dry mouth, he managed, "That's wonderful, Tracy will have a little sister, but I can't imagine after all these years we have tried to have a baby and then finally last year adopting Tracy. I just didn't think it would happen."

Just how could they afford another baby, he thought.

He was content with things just the way they were, besides it was hard for him to picture Stacy losing her figure even for a few months. He felt a tightness in his throat as he sat down and put his arms around his wife, holding her close. Somehow, he must maintain his composure. She had always admired his strength - his manliness.

He ran his fingers through his thick, closely cropped brown hair, aware that his wife was watching

him with that look she had when she came close to
reading his mind.

"You're awfully quiet, Clint. I get the feeling you
aren't happy with my news. I'm scared, after all Tracy
just has his first birthday last week."

Clint didn't answer. He also knew he was scared.
Speechless.

They clung together. He wished he could at least act
relaxed. It was hard for him to think of himself as a father
of two. What responsibility. Awesome.

Clint was an only child and had never felt deprived
in that role. Besides, his job as a shoe clerk didn't allow
him to suport a large family. True, he had worked in the
department for four years and next year was promised
head of the department. It was a secure position, people always needed shoes. He recognized the pain in the
pit of his stomach that he had the day his father died
from a heart attack.

Seven months passed quickly. Stacy looked lovely in
maternity clothing. She had a happy glow and a vibrancy
which had only been hinted at before.

"I've got news for you, it is not one baby."

Stacy and Clint chorused, "Not one baby?"

"There are three."

Clint heard Stacy say incredulously, "Three?"

For the first time in his life, Clint Stevens fainted.

Stacy was due in a week and Clint was called in to
see the store manager.

"Clint, I have been impressed with your dedication to
your work and your customer relations."

"Thank you, sir."

"I've been talking with the Board of Directors and
instead of promoting you to Dept. Head as we promised,
there is an opening for a store manager in Bangor, Maine.
If you want it, the position is yours."

Clint's mouth was dry and butterflies fought for freedom from his chest.

Again he managed, "Thank you, sir. How soon is this appointment in effect?"

"Four months, Clint. During that time I'll take you in my office and teach you the ropes."

He smiled at the young man, "I understand you are having a baby soon."

"Any day, sir, and not just one baby but three," Clint said proudly.

"Wow, you'll need a nanny for your children."

"Yes, my wife is worried how she'll cope with four babies under two."

"I've an idea."

The older man leaned backward in his chair.

"My daughter, Jenny, is graduating this spring from high school and, despite the urging of my wife and myself, she wants to take a year or two off before starting college. I could ask her how she would like to be your nanny."

"Wonderful."

How much Clint would have to tell Stacy when he got home. She would be thrilled about the promotion. What a change moving from California to Maine.

Arriving home, he found a scrawled note on the kitchen counter.

"I'm off to the hospital. They are on their way. Tracy is at Mother's."

Clint speeded the six miles to the hospital in his '92 Cutlass.

Entering the O.B. Wing of the hospital, he was met by a smiling nurse.

"Come with me, Mr. Stevens. You can scrub your hands and put on this gown so you can watch the babies' births."

Clint, as directed, donned the green gown and walked into the birthing room.

Stacy was working hard laboring, he thought.

She pushed in response to the nurse's command.

Holding her hand, he noted her forehead was moist as were her palms. Blonde hair escaped in a few ringlets from the scrub cap.

"One more push, honey."

"It's a girl," Dr. Swanson informed Clint.

Clint clung to the side of the birthing table as he heard, as from a great distance, "Another girl."

The room was swimming. He heard the nurse say, "Push a little harder, Stacy."

The third girl.

For the second time in his life, Clint Stevens fainted.

HIS ROYAL HIGHNESS

Dad bought a Montana bronco who had HR, with a bar underneath, branded deep into his left flank. He was a sorrel with the temperament to match. Unlike the three gentle and submissive horses who plodded ahead of the plow, this bronco was unpredictable and capricious. A barnyard maverick. He looked amazingly regal so we named him His Royal Highness but we called him HR.

Dad realized this mercurial animal must be traded because he needed four dependable workhorses. But until he made the trade, HR unofficially belonged to me.

I patted his head when I fed him his oats. I even sneaked him a sugar lump and sang when I stroked his neck. But when I attempted to curry his coat as well as his favor, he scorned my attentions with a well-placed kick.

I spent happy hours riding HR. I learned to lean forward in the saddle when he broke into a gallop. I spent as many happy hours fantasizing winning the Kentucky Derby. A truly amazing feat for a ten-year-old on an undisciplined bronco.

One day Mother packed Dad's lunch in a silver syrup pail and I was to ride HR and bring the lunch to the field. The silver metal caught the sun, frightening him and he bucked me over his head. I wore a sling, fashioned from a dishtowel, for weeks until my sprained ligament recovered. Worse, my parents forbade me to ride HR again.

Soon after my accident, Dad traded His Royal Highness for an ordinary but willing workhorse.

In my daydreams, I visualized him running free in the mountains of Montana, his white mane and tail regal in the wind.

AS STRONG AS STEEL

We liberated women are on the run but our panty-hose run faster. They self-destruct so rapidly that many of us wear several thousand pair in a lifetime.

Nylon hose were touted as "strong as steel and as delicate as a spider's web," when they were first marketed in 1938. This exquisite hyperbole was lethal enough to kill a silkworm.

Nylons came in one width, narrow, barely covering the knees of most women. Therefore, fearful of skin showing above her stockings, a lady crossed her legs at the ankle.

Thighs came out of hiding with the introduction of pantyhose. But the runs were not reduced. Who among us hasn't felt a run cascading the leg of her last pair of hose while dressing for an important event?

To whom do we turn for longer life nylons?

We can begin by writing our congresswomen to legislate nylon reform. Hosiery manufacturers must fulfill the promise that nylons are as "strong as steel and as delicate as a spider's web," in the next millennium.

MUCH ADO ABOUT TOOTHBRUSHES

I just returned from shopping. I bought two dozen toothbrushes for seventy-five percent off the original price. A marvelous bargain. It was great fun to pick out the colors—white, black, melon, purple, green and amber.

The amber brush reminds me of my father's toothbrush. This bacteria-laden atrocity was the only one I remember him using, its bristles as scarce as money during the Great Depression. Even scarcer than Dad's teeth, worn to nubbins over the years. He stored the brush propped in the medicine chest above the kitchen sink.

Although Dad was generous to a fault, he had a hangup on toothbrushes, feeling they should last a lifetime. He accused me of extravagance if I bought a new one every year or two. I remember a big argument when I replaced one after six months.

In spite of, or because of my early conditioning, I gradually became a toothbrush sophisticate using separate but equal brushes morning and evening. I diligently brush after each meal or snack. It keeps me from snacking at inconvenient times to brush.

My toothbrush shelf is awesome. I own two traveling brushes in quaint little cases. Other brushes have flexible heads or handles. I've tried most brands and keep a supply for guests in a rainbow of colors.

When I toss a toothbrush, guilt attacks. I keep them to clean woodwork and scrub jewelry. A toothbrush works well to clean dirt from the crevices of my golf shoes.

Sometimes, like my father, I keep a favorite amber toothbrush in a mug high on the medicine shelf.

DOORS

By the grace of God we:
Shut the door on the past—a past
which haunts us with its mistakes.
Shut the door on jealousy and envy.
Shut the door on unrealistic expectations.
Shut the door on hopelessness.
Shut the door on prejudice and bigotry.
Shut the door on the darkness of negativity.

By the grace of God we:
Open wide the doors of optimism and
forgiveness
to the sunshine of God's love for ourselves
and others.

PLUMP THE PILLOWS

How much time do you and I spend worrying about what others may think? These same others who worry about what you and I think. Wasted worrytime. Who of us can add a year to our lives by worrying about what others may think.

A sixty-year-old has lived for 31,536,000 minutes. Most people sleep eight hours a day; therefore, the average sixty-year-old has had 21,024,000 waking minutes and unlimited choices to make during those minutes. Vocational choices. Personal choices. These choices take energy.

Worry is wasted energy. For none of us can control what others may think or feel. It is their choice. Hitler attempted mind control and botched it. Others have tried it in more benign ways.

Mother worried about what others thought. A good homemaker, she wanted to be regarded as an excellent housekeeper. Therefore, when we saw a car entering our long driveway, she said, "Angie, there is a car coming."

This was my cue to plump the pillows on the blue flowered terrycloth daybed. There were seven pillows. Mother had embroidered one for every day of the week. They were always in disarray because I sprawled on the daybed while reading.

While I plumped the pillows, Mother banished the few things setting around in the kitchen to the pantry. Answering the knock on the kitchen door, she appeared in a clean apron, hair smooth, with a welcoming smile for the visitor.

As an adult, I perpetuated the neat house image. Before I entertained, toys, magazines and small junk vanished. I worried what the guest would think when I burned the roast or the lemon pie meringue wilted or the telephone rang with an urgent message as we were seated at the table.

However, our house had a living room which doubled as a gymnasium. Four boys romped and wrestled on the floor. There was no long driveway so when the doorbell rang, that was it.

Our sons or grandsons grow long hair and while we know the same gentle hearts beat in their chests and the same bright brains, although they may appear dormant, lie under that long hair, we worry what people will think.

I may change my hair color for fear others will think that I, too, am aging. I may change my hair style and makeup to create a new persona I find attractive. Will friends and family support this change in my appearance?

And clothes—fit, style and color. Are they becoming or only comfortable? I like bright colors but will people think that I should wear more subdued clothes?

What will they think if I regain those same ten pounds I lost last year? I could wear one of those new empire waist dresses which would mask it.

Older adults return to college. Some think college is only for the young and forget that the young in heart need to pursue new interests and develop new talents.

Many worry if they remarry soon after their mate dies. People may think they are dishonoring the memory of their former mate. Although a year is customary, it is not mandatory and if they are no longer young, life's clock is running faster.

A couple builds a house which accommodates their

lifetime treasures. But they are plagued by the nagging fear that friends think them foolish or extravagant.

I challenge you to live your life and to plump your pillows, not because of what others may feel or think, but to ensure your life is full of zest and contentment.

THE KITCHEN SLOP PAIL

My slop pail memories are so repulsive that I've buried them as deep as a landfill for more than fifty years.

Memories of potato peelings, eggshells and coffee grounds immersed in dishwater in a five gallon pail are not palatable.

This pail was nearly hidden under the water reservoir of the gray and white kitchen range. Out of sight when company came. That same company who hid their slop pail under their kitchen range.

I accidently dropped a fork into the murky liquid. Reaching up to my elbow into the bacteria-laden pail, I retrieved it. Mother boiled the fork for an hour and my hands were raw from three latherings of pink soap. This grimy water was, you guessed it, recycled to the slop pail.

In winter the potato peelings bubbled through the ice, making an intricate pattern on the ground, but the garbage attracted rodents so Dad created our personal landfill.

Summer and winter, each Saturday Mother scrubbed the slop pail with bleach. Nice smell.

Whenever I hear someone talk about the "good old days," I need only to retrieve my slop pail memories to refute them.

BITTERSWEET

"The biopsy is not benign."

The measured voice of the surgeon enables my mind to comprehend that word—cancer. The word takes on a life of its own which is to last for nine stomach-wretching months.

Escaping from the grim present, I think back to the events of the previous week. Tuesday, tired from lecturing to a roomful of student nurses about the classic symptoms of stomach cancer, I realize my husband appears to have these symptoms.

I think, *Hypochondria, the nurses' neurosis.*

"Honey, have a biopsy just to be safe."

Returning to the present, I hear my husband and his surgeon making plans for surgery. In one week.

My mouth is dry and tiny droplets form under my eyelids. The lump in my throat grows as large as an apple. My diamond sparkles on my damp palmed hand.

It is a week of sweetest communication interspersed with heartbreak—a future which is limited by the new persona in our household.

Bittersweet.

IN A FEW WORDS

It's amazing how word usage changes in a few years. Some words gain in popularity, while others wither on the literacy vine.

Incredible is the word of the day. I count its use during a television show. I don't hear unbelievable, impossible, inconceivable or improbable, only that pseudo-sophisticated word, incredible.

I find it incredible that I don't hear the word fantastic much more. It reached the top of the literacy hit parade twenty years ago. An explosive word. I can't imagine a passive person saying, "Fantastic!" with any emphasis. We have become more aggressive and less verbal during these twenty years, thus explosive words are out of fashion.

Harass is another catch word which has grown in usage. It sounds as ominous as its meaning. The hissing consonants grate on my ears.

Trouble is a musical negative word. Unlike harass, trouble doesn't hiss. Harass is the neighborhood bully word whereas trouble comes as a thief in the night. Silent. Unbidden.

Happiness hisses too. But it is a comfortable hiss. More like a teakettle. It is a word for all time.

Litigation is another up and coming word of the nineties. It is an interesting word composed equally of vowels and consonants. Five of each, fair treatment. Liberty and justice for all. Part of our constitution.

Does justice guarantee fair treatment? Justice is a

strong word conjuring up images of courtrooms, judges and juries. However, truth is not always served by justice. Albert Schweitzer said, "Truth has no special time of its own. Its hour is now—always." Truth is a sturdy and honest word. Boris Pasternak said, "In every generation there has to be some fool who will speak the truth as he sees it."

We weigh justice on a scale, we scale a wall, we track our weight on a scale. In school we practice the musical scale. Scale is a confusing and interesting word, a word of many definitions.

Prejudice is an ugly word. To recognize our own prejudices is the first step toward eliminating them.

Education is a grand erudite word. According to John Dewey, "Education is a social process . . . education is growth . . . education is not preparation for life; education is life itself."

One of my favorite words is friend. It has a mellow sound. Warm. A friend relieves loneliness. A friend makes life zestful.

Radiant is a glowing, incandescent word, personified by brides or new parents. A bright and joyous word.

The word abominable rolls off our tongue when describing an atrocity such as genocide or something as unpleasant as bad weather. It serves to separate us from the situation.

Peace. Reassuring and calm, of which Helen Keller said, "I do not want the peace which passes understanding; I want the understanding which bringeth peace."

Spendid is a wonderfully positive word I rarely hear. It is reminiscent of Old World splendor. A strong word. A word with class.

Words, as people, have personalities, some wise, some foolish, some kind and some cruel.

In reading literature from the turn-of-the-century, I see vast changes in word usage.

Entering the new millennium, it will be interesting to see new words emerge, used next to the grand old ones which have gained in wisdom throughout the ages.

VIETNAM MEMORIAL

A hushed crowd gathers
by the stark black wall of grief.
A wall of names memorialized by sorrow
and carved with anguish.
A wall baptized by rain
and consecrated by sunshine.
One black wall over ten foot tall,
riveting in its simplicity,
heals the broken soul of a nation.
The silent crowd moves on.

SEWING GENES

It all goes back to the genes. Forever the genetic factor. Sewing. Whether it started with my grandmother or grandmother's grandmother, who lived on the craggy cliffs of Norway, I have no way of knowing.

I do know my grandmother was one whiz with a needle. Embroidery or machine. Emigrating from Norway at the age of eighteen, she opened a dressmaker shop in a southern Minnesota town which was populated with Norwegian immigrants. The finest dressed ladies in town wore her clothes. Lace, satin, wool or cotton, they were lovely to look at and comfortable to wear. Custom creations.

After marriage she continued sewing. With a purpose. Four daughters were outfitted with her splendid creations. Their clothes as lovely as the daughters. Both daughters and clothes photographed well.

All four daughters sewed — it was preordained. Genetic. Mother sewed my sister's as well as my clothes. Many were madeover from clothes from her teaching days. She ripped the seams, pieced small pieces and repatterned them. All were lovely. She also made my school dresses from printed feedsacks. Colorful prints.

Not only did my grandmother, mother and aunts sew dresses, they also did handwork. Glorious handwork. Crocheted bedspreads, doilies and afghans. Knitted sweaters, coats, caps and mittens. Embroidered pillowcases, luncheon sets with hemstitched edges and dishtowels depicting ladies in ballgowns holding umbrellas.

Both Mother and Aunt Millie tried to teach me to knit. I preferred a pencil to a knitting needle in my hand. As for embroidery, one Christmas I, warned there was no money for presents, received a surprise gift. A sofa pillow. Its design stamped in indelible ink. Included were embroidery cotton and needles. I was ten years old and pretended to be thankful but I was no actress. Soon, with my help, the sofa pillow disappeared.

Grandma was a quilter. One lovely old quilt of rich velvet and wool is draped over the stair railing in my sister's home. Its rich red catches the early morning sun.

Mother also quilted. She frequently held quilting parties followed by dessert. Once, joining the ladies, I pricked my finger and made a large blood stain. Soon, Mother asked me to start the coffee. It was to have been my first as well as my last experience quilting.

For years I emulated Mother and sewed dresses and slacks, coats and suits, even my husband's and sons' shirts. Then I stopped abruptly. I gave my sewing machine to my granddaughter.

My sister sewed lingerie and ski clothes for her family. Then she, too, stopped sewing. As abruptly as I.

My home is full of wonderful genetic reminders. An offwhite afghan on my white sofa, a king-sized white popcorn crocheted bedspread covers the bed in our guest bedroom. A star quilt hangs on the wall in that same room. Grandma's flower garden quilt on the spare bed at the cottage.

My daughter-in-law has Grandma's treadle machine near the door. It holds caps and mittens, schoolbooks and treasures. Cozy and a reminder of days long past.

Although sewing appears to be genetic, it may have stopped with me. None of my sons show the slightest interest in sewing.

I just might give one of them a sofa pillow and embroidery thread for Christmas and see what happens.

OF DIARIES AND JOURNALS

Most of us lead busy lives, or like to think we do, and don't document our actions and adventures or our thoughts and feelings.

But if we did—a glorious record of our lives would endure. It would help generations after us understand the history of our time.

Our first diary is kept by our mother. A baby book. This baby book carefully documents our first "coo" and "goo" and our first step. Particularly if we are the first-born. It tells a story of recognizing mother as our primary caretaker but saying the first word to our father. It documents our first outings with our first friends.

We learn to print and later to write. We may receive a gift of a five-year diary with a lock and key. We write in a childish scrawl which tells of the happy times as well as the hurts of a young life, but mostly it records facts.

In high school we write about our first love. We write of second, even third loves. We write of the struggle to achieve academically while struggling for self-identity and self-worth.

We practice writing a sophisticated backhand, carefully dotting each i with a little round circle.

We write each day, hiding our diary from family and friends. Our secret life.

In college, our diary becomes a journal. Its pages record our activities with friends, the wonder of young adulthood, and our eagerness to start a career. We believe our generation will change the world. There will be peace and economic security for all. We write idealistically of plans for these changes.

Most of us marry and have children. Some of us juggle career and family. We come full circle with a baby book for each child, patiently documenting first steps and first words. We fill scrapbooks with momentoes. Photo albums burst with pictures—from kindergarten to high school and beyond.

Busy, we take little time to write about ourselves. Later our personal journal assumes priority. Lengthy dissertations center again on the self—its feelings of failures, sauced with success.

Much later we use these diaries and journals for autobiographical material or vignettes. A poem may emerge. Our diary unlocked, our lives are no longer secret.

I GET THE DASHER

Ice cream is a quintessential delight. Whether three scoops on the double cone of my childhood (the cones sold for five cents) or scooped like a pyramid into the honey waffle cone of today, it is a mouthwatering delicacy. From the age of nine months to ninety and nine years, we adore its creamy texture.

On Sunday winter afternoons, my parents froze ice cream. Mother cooked a custard from eggs, sugar and milk. After this mixture cooled, she added heavy cream, a dollop of vanilla and poured it into the shining silver ice cream bucket.

Then Dad packed a mixture of crushed ice and salt between the silver bucket and the wood jacket of the ice cream freezer. He placed the cast aluminum dasher into the creamy sweet liquid. This dasher, the free spinning heart of the freezer, whipped the cream as it froze. When my aunt, uncle and their five daughters came, an expected conversation materialized.

Uncle Carl asked Dad, "Ice cream frozen yet?"

Dad answered, "You are just in time to crank."

Each of my five cousins, my sister and myself, supervised by our fathers, took a turn at the crank. When the crank became too stiff to turn, Dad knew the ice cream was frozen.

We were rewarded for our efforts when he removed and held high the dasher. We stood expectantly around the freezer and fought over, then scraped and finally licked that most wonderful ice cream which clung to its blades.

Dad repacked the freezer with fresh ice and salt and left the ice cream to ripen. The soft ice cream looked like the present day soft serve, but when it sat in the cold freezer, it became so firm it required great strength to dish it up. The strength of that strong man, my father. To a child, the ripening seemed to take an interminable length of time. An hour seemed as a day.

Mother dished the vanila delight into green sherbet glasses. It was fun to trace the design around the rim of the glass with an ice cream sticky finger. It was even more fun to place our spoon in it and start eating.

My parents' ice cream was as cold as a Minnesota winter. Eating it caused a pain in my forehead. I ignored the pain because I adored ice cream.

I still adore ice cream and keep it as a staple in the deep freeze. At times it talks to me. Loud.

I shop for ice cream and find a mind-boggling array of low fat, no fat, fat free, sugar free in round, square, or oblong cartons. I pick out two half gallon cartons, one fat-free, sugar-free ice milk, thinking it will keep my weight and cholesterol within reason and the second carton of specialty ice cream. Its creamy texture, thick with fudge and nuts will test my willpower.

At the check-out counter my mind wanders back to an unsophisticated era when ice cream was a novelty. A wintertime desssert.

Each time I lick the spoon after dishing ice cream for dinner, I fantasize licking the dasher.

MEET YOU IN THE MELONS

I was in a carful of teen-agers before the word teen-ager was coined. Six of us were hurtling through the countryside at forty miles an hour when the driver slammed the brakes, jumped out of the car, and ran down the ditch over to a farmer's garden and returned with a huge dark green striped watermelon. Quickly, he cut it into pieces with his pocketknife and the six of us shared the glistening pink fruit. It was sweet, that forbidden fruit, scary, too. I was terrified that the farmer with his guard dog would find us. Then I would be an accomplice to a crime.

My parents had a watermelon patch on their farm, too. Dad stopped at the garden before the morning chores and cut a postage size "tester" in a melon to see if it was ripe. If ripe, he ate the whole thing.

I never raised watermelons. I just bought a large one each Fourth of July. My four boys ate it at the picnic table because previously I had found watermelon seeds tracked all over the house, the sweet sticky juice sticking to their shoes. My sons loved watermelon seed fights, taking a slippery black seed between thumb and first finger and letting it fly. Once I found a July watermelon seed while decorating a Christmas tree.

You don't need to go to Vegas to gamble—only to your supermarket to pick a melon.

Watermelons are the easiest to pick out. When you rap one with your knuckles and it sounds hollow, it's ripe. Colors range from pale yellow or pink to deep red. Cantaloupe are quite another story. If they have a liquid shake, they may be ripe or rotten, too close to call. I check the stem end and if it is soft, the melon is ripe. Maybe.

Honeydews are worse. I have never found a ripe one. But I keep trying.

Melons make a colorful and tasty fruit mixture. They abound in watermelon boats at graduations and summer patio parties.

I love cantaloupe and honeydew; however, I haven't enjoyed watermelon since that sweet stolen melon of my youth.

THE PERSISTENT SUITOR

That's the girl I'm gonna marry, Terry thought, when he saw Muriel and a girlfriend sitting on a large rock by Blue Eagle Lake.

His brother was right. Muriel Solum was the most beautiful girl in Barnesville.

His brother also added, "She rides a horse so often she probably smells like one."

Terry wasn't aware of any horse smell but he did notice her expressive blue eyes and lovely smile as well as the sweet swell of her breasts under the straps of her blue and white sundress when she stooped to select a flat rock to skip on the water.

Terry McGrath was fifteen going on sixteen and spending the summer of '40 with his uncle Jim Lakie and family in Barnesville. The Lakies lived down the street from the Solum home. Muriel, the eldest of five daughters, was nearly two years older than Terry.

Terry played on Barnesville's Junior Legion baseball team. He spent hours of batting practice hitting the leaves of an old elm tree in the Lakie's back yard while he watched Muriel suntan. Terry, smitten but shy, asked his brother Bernie to arrange a date with Muriel. It was to be the first of many dates that summer.

Before leaving, he told her, "I'll be back for your graduation and I hope we can go out afterward."

Home in Oregon, he told everyone in the high school about Muriel and that eventually he was going to marry her. Even as an adolescent, Terry was a goal setter.

He sat in the bleachers at the Barnesville High School graduation and, afterward, was the first to congratulate Muriel. However, the date was not to materialize.

"Sorry, Terry, I have a date for the dance with a classmate."

The two dated frequently during the summer. He never doubted they would one day marry. Terry was drafted for the navy after graduating from high school in 1943. Muriel completed three years of nursing; then, as an R.N., joined the Army Nurse Corps in March of 1945.

When the war ended in August 1945, both were serving in the Philippines. Later they served in the occupational forces in Japan; Terry aboard ship in the Tokyo Bay area and Muriel in a hospital in Kayto, the beautiful Japanese shrine city.

Terry obtained a leave to visit her during Christmas of 1945. They had not seen each other since the summer of 1941.

Muriel took his hand and said, "I'm so happy to see you, Terry, but I can talk with you for only fifteen minutes because I'm not to fraternize with an enlisted man."

Her charge nurse arranged to put Terry in a room of enlisted men for five days. He and Muriel were able to visit on several occasions.

Before leaving, he said, "Let's get married next summer in Barnesville."

Both were discharged during the summer of '46. Soon

after, Terry received a letter from Muriel.

"I think it's nice you're coming to Barnesville to see your relatives but if you are coming to see me, don't bother."

Terry was not easily discouraged.

His Dad encouraged him, "Terry, you aren't worth a damn but you'll never get straightened out until you go to Barnesville and see Muriel."

Muriel was living at the Pelican Lake cottage with her parents and sisters so Terry made arrangements to stay on the same beach with his aunt.

He wore the grass bare between the two cottages. The summer went quickly and in a week he planned to go home and attend Oregon State University.

Saturday night, on Labor Day weekend, while dancing at the Detroit Lakes Pavilion, Muriel stepped back two feet and said, "Terry, if you still want to marry me, we could get married a week from tomorrow."

They didn't finish the dance.

On the telephone from Oregon, his dad commented to Muriel, "I knew Terry was a damn fool but I didn't know you were, too."

Sept. 8, 1946, Terry and Muriel were married at Our Savior's Lutheran Church in Barnesville.

Muriel smiled at Terry as she walked down the aisle escorted by her father. She wore a dress made from the silk she had purchased in Japan, handmade that week by her mother.

Terry had never seen anyone as beautiful as his bride.

The next morning, the newlyweds left for Oregon.

Much later, Muriel was to admit, "In Japan, I had a dream about you. I woke up and told my roommate, 'I'm going to marry Terry McGrath.' "

FROM PAINT CHIP TO WALL

I belong to a family of do-it-yourself painters. Sharing the same genetic flaw, we choose the wrong paint color 50 percent of the time, thus we have become masters of repainting.

My folks changed the color of their kitchen after a sheet-twisting, pillow-flipping night for the paint chip named apricot looked as orange as a highway sign on the wall. It took two coats of pastel blue to hide it.

Pastel blue repaint jobs run in our family. My aunt covered the vivid green of her family room the day after her sleepless night.

At my lake cottage, worn by time, repairs are as routine as washing dishes.

I changed the brown plywood kitchen cabinets to a rich gold semigloss. It took two strokes of the brush before I made an emergency trip to the hardware store for a safer spring green. The bile green deck paint came to the same bitter end. A non-obstrusive gray helped my nausea.

Sometimes the paint and I peacefully co-exist. The beautiful beige paint on the cottage turned a pale pink as it dried. Later, with new owners, it was painted a boat-cover blue. In the winter startling, but stunning with the summer greens.

My sister, who has an interior design business, learned from the family mistakes and advises clients to first try a small can of paint in their favorite paint chip color.

The rest of us continue to paint and repaint.

JUST SUBSTITUTE SODA

I see baking soda is featured in television commercials as diverse as toothpaste and scouring powder.

A little soda goes a long way. It tastes bitter.

I didn't realize soda went such a long way until, enrolled in nursing school, I decided to bake a cake for my friends. Short of flour, I substituted—you guessed it—baking soda. It was a lovely white layer cake. High and handsome. I covered its sides and top with brown sugar frosting, then backed away to admire its elegance. I made coffee and set the table with four chipped and cracked blue and white cups. In the center of the table I placed the cake.

My friends were impressed with the delicate white cake and its brown fluffy frosting so each took a large slice. The aftertaste showed by their soda-shocked expressions.

"Soda—phew," they chorused.

"What did you do to this cake?"

"I just substituted soda for flour."

With that misadventure, I lost my reputation as a baker; no one asked for my recipe and I didn't offer.

It was to be a never-to-be-forgotten cake. Twenty-five years later at a class reunion, laughter turning to tears, they remembered "Angie's soda cake."

I am amazed at advertisements claiming soda as the secret ingredient. For the soda in my cake was no secret!

THE BIRTHING OF A POEM

My mind races
changing half-formed thoughts
to distilled phrases.
My pencil flies,
it bypasses my head
and concentrates on finger thoughts.
A poem is born.

ALL MY EGGS IN ONE BASKET

"Put all your eggs in one basket, and watch that basket."
Mark Twain

Mother was a baker with cheeks rosy under her glasses from being too close to the wood-burning kitchen range. I, her errand girl, often biked three miles over rolling hills to Rollag Store.

This time it was for eggs. Mother's treasured chocolate cake, red from the melted unsweetened chocolate beat into the egg and sugar batter, required four eggs.

Bernice, with her cheery smile, counted twelve eggs and placed them in a brown paper bag in exchange for the fifteen cents which I clutched in the sweaty palm of my left hand. I placed the brown bag in my bike basket and pedaled up and down the hills with the speed which comes from the energy of the young.

I loved Mother's chocolate cake and thought of it often during the ride home.

To my horror, the bottom of the bag was wet and sticky and all but two eggs dropped out of that brown bag and splattered on the newly washed floor.

Ten eggs at my feet.

Fifteen cents wasted.

Mother cheerfully cleaned the egg mess and said, "You'd better go back for another dozen."

I did. Bernice triple bagged the eggs. This time it took three times longer to bike home for I held the sack carefully in my left hand while steering with my right. All twelve eggs arrived home safely.

This childhood experience taught me the value of the old saying, "Don't put all your eggs in one basket." The bottom may drop out and all will be lost.

Make friends of people from different cultures and races. Your life will be enriched and you will learn from them.

Continue to make new friends—especially as you grow older—your contemporaries may die and unless you replace them with new friends you will be lonely. Consider friends of all ages.

Learn a new skill on a regular basis, even if you don't become proficient, you will keep interested in the future.

Diversify investments. If one turns sour the rest may retain value.

Make a plan for your future but have a contingency plan in case the sack of eggs breaks.

Renew your faith daily. Even if all your eggs drop from the basket, God's love will sustain you.

MOVING OF
THE HOLY SPIRIT

Beyond my imagination
Your love for me
Beyond my knowledge
Your concern for me
Beyond my expectations
Your plans for me

Beyond your expectations
His love for you
Beyond your knowledge
His concern for you
Beyond your expectations
His plans for you

Beyond our imagination
Your love for us
Beyond our knowledge
Your concern for us
Beyond our expectations
Your plans for us

THE LIBRARY TABLE

My living room furniture is grouped around the century old library table which my parents, newlyweds, bought at a household action to furnish their home.

Mother taught me to read and write on this table before I started school. I remember years of homework sitting at this table, looking out the window at the lilacs, heavy with snow in winter and turning pink with blooms in the spring. A daydreamer, I tipped my inkwell, leaving a stain as blue as denim on its golden oak surface. I stored small treasures in its one small drawer.

Later, Mother refinished the table and the inkspot was removed from its high gloss surface. It sat in her bedroom covered with family pictures.

Now it sits in front of my window and supports my pictures, awaiting a new generation of readers and writers.

WATERWITCH

Long ago I made a vow never to wash clothes on Monday morning. Any other day of the week but never on a Monday. I am haunted by Monday morning memories.

My happy and cheerful mother was never happy or cheerful on washday. She didn't look her usual pretty self either, wearing an ill-fitting print housedress with a neckline called sweetheart, low on her bosom. Her dark brown hair, thick with bobby pins, was pulled tightly off her face and fastened behind her ears. Her shoes, run down at the heels and worn only on washday, were a shoemaker's nightmare.

Gloom settled over our household like the heap of dirty clothes lying on the kitchen floor. Early in the morning, Dad pulled the green gas washer, aptly named Waterwitch, into the middle of the kitchen floor, the exhaust hose out the door. He also carried in pails of water from the pump, located some fifty feet from the house, and filled the copper boiler waiting on the kitchen range.

That same range sported a large aluminum kettle with a three-to-four pound chunk of soup meat immersed in water. In between loads of clothes, Mother chopped vegetables for the soup and the pot simmered all morning on the back burner.

Our dog, Patsey, hid behind the range on Monday mornings.

A housewife was judged by the whiteness of her clothes and Mother's wash sparkled. Even her embroidered feedsack dishtowels had no stains. She removed coffee stains with cold water and fruit stains with boiling water.

All whites were washed first in hot water fortified with shaved homemade soap and household bleach. Colored clothes, towels and Dad's workclothes and socks followed, always in the same order. After the clothes were agitated, they were removed with an old broomstick and hand cranked through a wringer, first into a tub of clear water, followed by a tub of blue water. The first white clothes were bluing blue which soon bleached in the sun.

Mother made a light starch by pouring a cup of corn starch into a shallow yellow crock. She mixed this with cold water and when smooth, poured boiling water from the teakettle until the solution became transparent. It was the same technique she used while making her lemon pie filling except the clothes starch had no lemon or sugar. Tasteless.

Our cotton dresses and Dad's white shirt collar were carefully starched. She was especially careful of Dad's shirt collar as he had only one white shirt.

It was my duty to carry out the pails of blackened water and pour them on the pink petunias near the kitchen door. The petunias thrived with this care.

Mother and I hung the clothes on rope lines tied to the trunks of the boxelder trees in our backyard. The clothes were segregated on the line. Whites from colored. First sheets, followed by dish towels, bath towels, dresses, trousers and finally socks matched by color, two to a clothespin. These clothespins were confined to an orange canvas bag on a wire hanger which we pulled along the line as we hung up the clothes.

Often the clotheslines broke and the clothes, half-buried in the dirt, were dirtier than before they were washed. We two washerwomen rewashed the clothes and pinned them to the retied rope line, hoping no bird would fly over and leave its droppings.

On winter days, Mother and I draped the clothes over three wooden clothes racks in the porch. The clothes froze dry and the next day we carried them, stiff as boards, into the house. The dampness provided a welcome humidity as well as a wonderfully clean, fresh smell.

Between washdays, I made a cozy playhouse in the living room by covering the clothes racks with two blue and white seersucker bedspreads. I placed a motheaten green wool robe on the floor. Some weeks, when the snow was deep and company not expected, Mother allowed me to keep the playhouse until the next washday. It was, in turn, my tent, my igloo, my boat or my castle.

Summer or winter, by noon the laundry was done and we ate dinner, the traditional vegetable beef soup. Carrots, peas, potatoes and parsnips floated on the greasy broth. No crackers. I preferred mine without the homemade brown bread.

Mother and her sisters learned to make the Monday soup from my grandma. Later, in Homemakers, Mother learned to chill the soup and skim the fat before serving.

After the waterwitch was cleaned and wheeled into the far corner of the kitchen and covered with a red and white checked oilcloth until the next Monday morning, Mother took a well-deserved nap. She snored with delicate little puffs for a mere twenty minutes but it was a lonely twenty minutes for me. I turned the radio loud to awaken her. This worked well.

After Mother's nap, we took down the clothes and folded them carefully into the wicker basket. We made the beds with the sweet-smelling sheets.

Although I remember those fresh sheets fondly, I never wash clothes or make soup on a Monday.

BARNS

I have had long and tempestuous love affairs with more than one barn. I first fell in love with a log barn at age five. It was the first building I noticed when we moved to the farm for it stood between our house and the road. I spent happy hours playing in the white-washed log building.

It was in turn my castle, my boat, and my home. It had many small rooms in which I could hide. The narrow cracks between the logs were windows through which I watched the barn sparrows build their nexts and the squirrels race up a nearby boxelder tree.

The carpenters came to build a new barn. An enormous pile of sand in our backyard provided a great place to play, Daily the sandpile was transformed into concrete and my log playbarn was replaced by a bright red new barn. The new barn also had many places for me to hide. It smelled of new lumber and horses. Even the cattle became my friends. I named all five of them, Molly, Annie, Nellie, Rosie and Christie.

As I grew older, I imagined barn dances in the empty hay loft. There were men and women in western attire, clothing pictured in the Sears catalog. Men in fringed, leather jackets and women in red and blue wide swirling skirts. I had never seen anyone dance but as I shut my eyes to see them gracefully circle the empty hay loft, I, dressed, in mother's discarded dress, twirled with them.

I wrote long love letters to my boyfriend. The

boyfriend who wasn't aware he was a boyfriend. Then I hid the letters under the eaves, little pockets on all four sides of the barn. Wonderful hiding places. I expect the letters are still there waiting to be read. For the barn stands proudly on my cousin's farm. Still red. Still smelling of hay and cows. Someday I'll look in that barn, under those eaves for those old letters.

Barns, as people, come in all shapes and sizes. Round, oblong and square. Barns with painted logos. Red barns with shingle roofs. White barns. Barns with a leanto attached.

Some barns shelter more horses than cows. I call them horse barns. Some barns had only cows, they are dairy barns—unusually clean barns. Many Wisconsin barns have murals painted on them, beautiful scenes of rural America. Barn art galleries. A gift to tourists.

I love beautifully kept barns and falling down neglected barns, but I especially love hollow barns which catch the whistle of the prairie winds. For years I planned to photograph one such hollow barn, near Pelican Lake. The very day I took my camera in the car to take the picture—I'm not kidding—it had blown down the night before, the roof flattened on the ground.

I photograph barns from the car. Some are disappointing for they are but dots on the horizon of my pictures. When I use my zoom lens, I park the car by the side of the road to compose the picture.

Every year as I travel, I find fewer barns. They are replaced by steel machine sheds with no personality. Only hard unyielding metal. A far cry from the picturesque log barn of my childhood.

Recently I bought a book on barns a beautiful book depicting barns in the United States. It is surprising how the barns differ from coast to coast, showing the diversity of our country and cultures. A wide assortment from the different ethnic backgrounds.

The author, a kindred spirit, perhaps had an imaginary girlfriend whose love letters were hidden under the eaves of a barn. Perhaps he, too, had imaginary barn dances. Perhaps he was known to me in another life. Barn raising and barn dancing were in another life. A splendid life which only existed in my imagination.

CHRISTMAS EVE

It is December 24th, the day before Christmas, and I am ten years old and joyful for tonight I will receive a dolly. I know, because I have found her hiding place high on the shelf of Mother's closet. Placing an orange crate on top of the old brown trunk, I climbed high enough to reach that top shelf. I pushed aside a blanket and found a rectangular brown box with DOLL stamped on the outside. My conscience, or a fear of being caught, disallowed even one peak inside the box.

My dolly! Her name will be Annabelle and I can hardly wait to hold her. I wonder, as all prospective mothers, will she be blonde and blue-eyed or a brunette like me? I wonder if there are any red-haired dolls.

This Christmas Eve, as always, Mother bakes lefse. She rolls the potato bread dough in several large circles and bakes them on top of the black kitchen range, flipping them pancake fashion when they turn a pale freckled tan.

I devour one hot off the stove and roll it with butter and brown sugar, savoring its goodness. Later, at supper, it is served with the lye-cured codfish we Norwegians call lutefisk.

I grow increasingly excited when Dad, his face red from wind and snow, carries in a freshly cut evergreen and places it in a small alcove in the living room. A gust of wind enters with him.

"Blizzard conditions," he says.

Our little house is warm and snug and the scent of pine permeates its corners.

We have, the three of us, a friendly argument over what is the best side of the tree. We turn the irregular side against the wall. Mother and I trim the tree. Small treasures from earlier years, such as the little blue and silver bird, are fastened on its branches. Every year there are fewer and fewer feathers on his tail.

I slip red, blue, and white candles into the shining silver holders that fasten like a clothes pin to the branches of the tree. I am careful because a neighbor's house burned last year from a forgotten candle. Strings of popcorn and cranberries complete the decorations.

Mother places a lone package under the tree. It is a rectangular box wrapped in white tissue with lumpy corners and tied with a slightly frazzled silver ribbon carried over from last year's present. My package! There is little money this Christmas and no other packages under the tree. My parents only share the gift of their love.

Dad scratches a long wooden match with his well-worked farm hands and lights each candle until the room is transformed by their glow, and I know now that it is Christmas Eve. I try to keep from looking constantly at that silver and white package. Silver and white remind me of angels.

Dad opens the Bible to read the Christmas story. He opens it, oh-so-slowly, and reads from St. Luke, "And it came to pass in those days..."

In spite of myself, my eyes stayed glued to the package. I think that it is a long Bible reading. *Will he ever stop reading? Will Annabelle look like me?* We sing *Silent Night*, all three long stanzas.

Finally, Mother hands me my package.

"Here, honey. Merry Christmas."

Exuberant, I try not to rip the tissue too fast and I try to carefully remove the frayed silver ribbon to preserve it for next year's package.

Finally, I glimpse Annabelle. Resplendent in her pink satin dress and her little black patent shoes, she is unbelievably beautiful. Her eyes open when she sits up and they close when she lies down. Her ever-constant smile reveals shiny white teeth and a little pink tongue. Her hair is as dark a brown as my own. My dolly!

The smell of wax filters through the living room as Dad pinches off the flaming candles seconds before the fire could attack the tree's branches.

There is joy and peace and love in our little house. Even the wind has stopped blowing. I sing, "Sleep my child and peace attend thee, all through the night," as I sit in my brown wicker rocker and hold Annabelle. Both of us are content.

AN ASSORTMENT OF
CHRISTMAS TREE MEMORIES

I get tangled in tinsel when I sort out my Christmas tree memories. It is as looking in a box of old pictures, pausing too long over each so the task never gets done.

Chasing a flat frozen Christmas tree is like playing the market, you're never sure you made the right choice. It is a surprise when the branches thaw into place. The experts recommend a fresh cut on the trunk which is difficult unless you are adept with an ax or a saw. Soaking the tree in water a few days is even more difficult because from Grandma to Grandson, everyone is eager to start the trimming.

Trimming the tree, like dressing for a party, is exciting. One makes up with tinsel and accessorizes with ornaments. A small silver and blue bird, treasured from my childhood, stands on one leg - its tail feathers askew. I remember red, pink, green and yellow candles secure in embossed tin holders dripping wax on the ornaments. We watched the tree carefully when the candles were burning for Christmas tree fires were fearsome events.

Each year our family held a conference to ascertain the character and personality of the tree. An extroverted tree, comfortable in its exhibitionism, stood with red and green lights flickering in front of the window. The introverted tree, most comfortable with family and close friends, stood alone in a corner. Its blue lights symbolic of that first Christmas.

Some years the Christmas tree is small and scrubby. Other years it wears branches grown wide for nesting birds. Strangely, the presents under the scrubby tree were meager. They were wrapped in white tissue and tied with a frazzled silver ribbon. Whereas, under the barely-clearing-the-ceiling tree, the presents were glorious, such as new skates or a cranberry chenille robe with matching slippers. But they, too, were wrapped in white tissue and tied with the same tired ribbon, constants in an ever-changing Christmas world.

My husband and I come from differing tree camps. I favor a Norway pine alive with bristles. He prefers a symmetrical nonalive artificial tree. We fought before we bought the plastic tree. Soon he tired of storing and setting it up. We agreed to give it and the decorations to a family who were thrilled to have a Christmas tree. With love, I enclosed the silver bird from my childhood.

A friend has a yearly tree trimming party. Invitations to her party are treasured. After the Christmas tree is lit, she serves a homemade clam chowder and cherry pie supper. But best of all is our friend's lively hospitality.

Next year I plan to get to the bottom of my box of Christmas tree memories—sorting the past from the present. But for now I am enjoying the mix.

SUPERMARKETS AND SUCH

I met my husband at the supermarket. No, not among the peanuts and the peaches, but at the lunch counter. I asked, "How's the fish?"

"Fine, just fine."

Six months later we were married.

Interesting people abound in supermarkets. Like the woman with an agonized expression when dozens of her coupons flew as chicken feathers on the floor. I helped her pick them up but she didn't offer me a reward. I could have used the 35 cent coupon off my favorite coffee, especially as it was a triple coupon day.

She wasn't as talkative as the fellow I met in apples juggling Jonagolds.

Advancing toward me, he said, "Have you ever seen anything as big as these apples?"

Then, he, Adam, offered me, Eve, an apple.

I looked behind me with apprehension. No snake. However, to be safe, I never touched that apple.

You can tell alot about a person in a grocery store. Take the woman I met in eggs. One cautious lady. She opened at least nine cartons before one was just right. I edged carefully by her in case she encountered the same problem as the coupon lady.

She reminded me of my grandmother who always pinched the peaches. It wasn't a gentle touch to see if the peach was soft. But a cruel pinch. I was always glad my grandmother didn't use the same technique on me. Of course, I didn't meet her for the first time at the fruit market. Good thing, I may not have passed the pinch test.

The woman checking the size and weights of various brands of canned pears had much the same problem as the man who wanted only perfectly ripened pears. Perfectionists. I waited impatiently for them to make up their minds.

I wish I had a dime for every time I've seen someone crack and eat a peanut, leaving the shell for me. I notice most peanut poachers walk away without buying any.

Next time a friend complains there are no eligible men, I'll take her to the cheese department.

She can pick out a nice round red cheese and ask the first ringless male, "Have you ever tried Edam?"

She just might make a new friend. Like when I met my husband eating Minnesota walleye.

MY PIANOS

I've always had a nonreciprocal love affair with a piano. It all started when at six or seven I learned to play "Doctor, Doctor, Can You Tell?" on the church piano, while my friends were scurrying around the altar playing hide and seek.

Then I really got serious and at age eleven bought my first piano. Dad and I, armed with the fifty dollars I'd earned from milking the family cow, took a trip to the city for the purpose of buying a piano. We did. The most piano for your money possible; a huge upright, formerly a player piano with its innards scooped out. It had a much varnished magahony case and dingy yellow keys.

But I was happy. Not so my mother. She thought it the most ugly piece of furniture ever she did see. Even when she hung the multi-colored "radio scarf" with fringes on it and covered the top with family pictures, the piano still looked its age and sounded even worse.

I took a year of piano lessons while a freshman in high school and played "Hawaiian Nights" at the recital. A glorious performance.

My next love affair with a piano was with a pretty little walnut spinet. With good legs. Two sons took lessons and played well. Every time I played "Hawaiian Nights" they would say, "Shut the windows, shut the doors, Mom is playing."

My current love affair with a piano is with a black highly polished upright. It looks beautiful and I think it sounds great when I play my favorite, "Hawaiian Nights." One of these days I'll see if I can remember "Doctor, Doctor, Can You Tell?" But first, I'll shut my doors and windows.

SELF-IMAGE

Nature crashing,
words unleashing,
defenses stripped,
and ego shrieking,
is this the self called I?

Stranger, alien yet familiar
Does the crashing of the timber
still the sky of God's great splender,
is this the self called I?

No, it is a calm defender,
feminine and tender,
reaching upward to the sky,
grasping sunlight from the sender,
this self called I.

OF ICE CREAM AND OLD MAIDS

Two sisters, Alma and Grace, were co-owners of the Ice Cream Shop in the Barnesville of the forties. Their shop became a haven for high school students. Although between the two of them they had had three husbands, the students renamed both the shop and its owners "The Old Maids."

These sisters complemented each other. Grace, with hair the color of her hamburger spare chili, was the disciplinarian. Alma comforted the lovelorn and lonely, becoming a surrogate mother of many.

After basketball games, jostling students overflowed the five plywood booths. The rest of the fans stood, as thick as plush carpet, in front of the ice cream freezer.

The noise stopped when the Trojans entered, wearing their purple and gold letter jackets. Each made the round of the bulging booths and, regardless of the outcome of the game, were given a royal welcome.

Often Grace of the bobbed chili hair became ruffled by the confusion. She dished her discipline as quickly as if she were scooping ice cream for a walking sundae. A walking sundae was an ice cream cone topped with chocolate or caramel.

After the movie at the Bijou, dates gathered at the Old Maids. Self-concious first daters shared booth space with steadies.

Years later, I visited the widows after they opened a larger, classier restaurant in a neighboring town. But they weren't the same and neither was I.

A STEP BACK IN TIME

"You can't step into the same water twice."
Heroditus

I don't believe that District 14 Clay County, Minnesota has burned to the ground so I set out on an expedition to prove that it stands as stately and sturdy as it remains in my memory.

I leave Pelican Lake on the Lake Ida road. This road is wider and the hills not as high as I remember. I step on the gas at the apex of the hogsback as Dad did to give us a thrill. No thrill. Driving by the site of my childhood home, only the lilacs are familiar.

I see two ominous signs at the entrance of the road to the school. "Dead End," and "Minimal Maintenance Road—Enter at Your Own Risk."

Taking a deep breath, I risk boldly and turn my car onto the dead end road. This road, always adventuresome driving, is now but a trail through the high prairie grasses.

I arrive at a lonely place. No sign of the once proud school, its silver metal siding glistening in the sun. Only a few cottonwoods stand, rusty from their years.

Sitting alone in this place, I relive those sixty-year-old memories.

Silver District #14, a one-room country school built by Norwegian immigrants stands on an acre of land.

"A mile-and-a-half from nowhere," my father says, giving directions to the school.

The rectangular tin sheathed building is capped with an oversized bell tower and visible over a mile from the road. This road is blocked by heavy snow during the winter so that the school is accessible only by skis and sleds. Often I huddle under a brown horsehair robe, with its warm red wool lining, while Dad struggles to free the shivering team of horses, half buried in the snow.

A reporter from *The Forum* visits our school and writes a Sunday feature about our skiing prowess. Our teacher, with her thirty-three students, poses for a picture, our skis propped beside us against the schoolhouse wall.

My skis, handmade of oak, are wide at the front and narrow at the back. They are fast skis if my feet remain controlled by the black leather strap over my overshoes but many times both skis slide off and race ahead of me down the hill.

But in the fall and spring we walk to school. In the spring little ponds are formed from the melting snow. These ponds freeze overnight to form a thin ice we call rubber ice. It is high adventure to see how far we can walk out on the pond before the ice breaks. I roll up my long gray underwear and roll down my heavy brown stockings to enjoy the warm spring breezes. I always roll the underwear and the stockings into place before I arrive home.

This one-room school with its beige wainscoted walls is dominated by a faded print of George Washington. His eyes follow me whenever I even think of mischief. A sad-eyed Abe Lincoln keeps a melancholy presence. Our teacher's desk stands on a platform in front of the blackboard. Next to her desk, a pre-World War I dingy green globe hangs suspended from a pulley. Six oak chairs are grouped in a circle preparatory for class recitation.

To a first grader, the stove is enormous and more than a little frightening with its black jacket covering its round hot belly. To an eighth grader, the stove means work for a bucketful of coal is heavy. The stove's black jacket makes a convenient drier for caps, mittens and, on occasion, wet stockings.

Bookshelves hold an assortment of books from which I fashion daydreams—*Fairy Tales* by Hans Christian Andersen, Louisa M. Alcott's *Little Women* and the *Anne of Green Gables* series but my favorites, the red encyclopedias, stand alone, elegant on their black metal stand. They make splendid escape reading. It is to be many years before I will recognize their educational value.

Desks are assigned according to the grade, not the size of the pupil. The recessed glass inkwells prevent huge spills but my pen drips ink. Wiping the ink spot with a cloth makes the spot lighter in color but larger in circumference. Therefore, my desktop is the color of faded overalls.

I spend much of my study time inventing word codes as I never can talk mother into buying Ovaltine so I can order an Orphan Annie secret decoder ring. I could kill for Ovaltine. I hurry home to hear *Little Orphan Annie* at 4:45 on the radio, never guessing that Daddy Warbucks is political satire.

What our school lacks in equipment is compensated by the enthusiasm and energy of its teachers. These young women are groomed for rural teaching at a state teachers' college.

My first grade teacher is not only pretty with her red

hair and freckles, but patient and nurturing. We are five lucky first graders who adore her. I am even luckier as she boards at our house.

My middle elementary teacher also roomed at our house. Curious when she goes out on her first date with the young man she will later marry, I watch, hidden behind the living room drapes, as he hands her into his car. I wonder what it will be like to go out on a date.

All of the teachers wear dresses. Our sixth grade teacher wears a beautiful navy suit with a pink ruffled blouse framing her face. We girls wear dresses too. Mine are handmade (not homemade) by my mother.

My seventh and eighth grade teacher believes that if we set our goals we can accomplish anything we want in life. She is an experiential teacher, teaching grammar and social studies with a student newspaper published monthly. I carry the paper home in my dinner pail so it smells like oranges. The last week of school we have a smores and grapefruit juice breakfast at which each of us makes a commitment to keep in touch with her.

At 9 A.M. our teacher pulls the rope to ring the bronze bell hanging in the bell tower. Each day begins with the pledge of allegiance after which an eighth grade boy carries the flag to the flagpole. At 4 P.M. the flag is carefully furled and returned to the schoolroom. Classes in reading, arithmetic, history and geography for each grade are held every day. For remedial or enrichment learning, a student has only to tune into the class at will. Art is a Friday afternoon project. It ranges from embroidery to woodwork. I make bookends and give them a second coat of paint before the first one is dry. I find out that I am not an artist.

We also discuss our *Current Event* and *Weekly Reader* papers on Friday afternoons. We read about the first transcontinental air flight from New York to California. In my imagination, I am a frequent flyer.

Recess and noon hour are welcome. Each week, sides are chosen for the softball games we call kittenball. Care is taken to protect the youngest players from the pitcher's ball, but the pitching is relentless for the older students and many are out at the count of three. A few walk. Homeruns are cheered by both teams.

A large pencilbox is a status symbol. They are made of red or blue cardboard with a button clasp. The largest pencilboxes have three removable penciltrays and as many as six drawers. I am in the eighth grade before I acquire a red six-drawer beauty which I display atop my desk with a total lack of humility.

Valentine's Day is another indication of popularity and status. A large white box covered with red hearts is displayed for a week. Finally, at 2 p.m. February 14, we have a party with red nectar and cookies. Valentines are delivered by the King and Queen of Hearts. Coming from a non card-playing family, I had never heard of that royalty. The valentines range from red hearts made from construction paper to large cutouts proclaiming "I love you." Some hold a red sucker or a small candy bar. A few are made of paper doily lace with a Victorian message. I wait until I am home before I count my valentines. My favorite says, "You're a cute little devil and right on the level."

Little children smell and not only of soap and water. First graders innocently emit an earthy odor; sometimes older boys do too, but not as innocently. Older girls smell of sweet pea or lilac cologne after the Christmas vacation.

Paste smells too. A huge jar lasts the term, if dispensed frugally, and if we run out we make a homemade flour and water paste which, if forgotten on a dish, hardens into a crust.

Vomit has its own characteristic stomach churning smell which lingers for hours. There is no refrigeration so some of the vomiting may be caused by food poisoning.

Sweeping compound has its own unique smell. It is sprinkled liberally over the floor at the daily cleanup by the older students who take turns pushing the well-worked warehouse broom. They learn to toss out the compound and dust with the wind at their back to avoid the taste of grit.

Our school is not quiet. Sounds of more than five dozen restless feet, as well as whispers and giggles and the occasional sound of tears, raise the decibel level.

The Christmas program is the social event of the season. Parents, siblings and friends fill the small building. The door and windows are decorated with red and green construction paper wreaths. Desks sparkle with handmade decoration. Even my desk looks pretty.

A thin green curtain hangs on a clothes line forming the stage. Backstage the moments before performance are hectic. The curtain sways with restless feet showing beneath the curtain. All of us have some part in the program, some in group singing or solos, and others have recitations. Most popular are the one-act plays called Dialogues. Following the program, cookies and nectar are served. The nectar leaves red rings around the mouths of the preschool children.

We always receive a gift from our teacher. My favorite, a narrow gold embossed box contains three pencils. Each pencil has my name printed on it. I never sharpen these pencils beyond my name because I like to see it in print.

Hot lunches consist of each student bringing a small jar of food to be heated in a basin of water on the two-burner kerosene stove. There is a variety of lunches, from macaroni hotdish to creamed peas. Often we hear an explosion when a jar breaks and its contents spill into the swirling water. I notice the peas always float on top of the water.

The water fountain, a large earthenware crock, is filled each morning with water from the pump. Water comes from a spigot activated by a lever which creates a fountain. The residual water runs into a pail placed under the crock. One boy always drinks with a wad of bread tucked into his cheek. The rest of us avoid the fountain at the sight of those soggy crumbs.

Our school has its bad days and good, exciting days intermingled with boring days; but unlike the dead end road sign, it is the beginning, not the end of our lives.

Surprised to find that I have spent more than two hours immersed in the memories of my country schooldays and coming to terms with my own rusty roots, I back my car past those scraggly cottonwood trees onto this little traveled road.

GRAY MORNING

This morning my pencil won't write.
The sky is cold and uncompromising.
My feet are cold,
the coffee bitter.
Thoughts crowd into a crowded head.
My pencil lead breaks,
its sharpener lost.
I see a faint red streak
under a cloud
and await the sunrise.
I cook fresh coffee
and find a new pencil.
It writes of these crowded thoughts
from a crowded head.

FRIENDS OR FOES
THE DOGS IN MY LIFE

The heroism of the cocker spaniel/German shepherd who jumped into the family swimming pool to rescue the 21-month toddler, swimming under him and pulling him to safety, made heartwarming front page news.

None of the dogs I've known have made the front page but my cousin Muriel's dog was a hero, too. A delightful pug-nosed bulldog hero. Muriel and Monk were crossing the street and he dashed between her and an oncoming car. Monk was killed and the car missed Muriel by a millisecond.

Shep, our farm watchdog, was no hero. He had a nasty disposition and greeted all visitors with a snarl. Shep nipped at my legs while I was playing with him and a couple of days later he was no longer around. To this day, I don't know or care what happened to him.

Patsey, a friendly collie resembling Lassie, was my best dog friend. I spent a week at my cousin's lake cottage and one afternoon I started to cry because I knew something had happened to Patsey. The next day my parents arrived to take me home. Mother looked strange when I told her my fears about Patsey.

"It must have been a premonition," she said as she put her arms around me. "She choked to death yesterday afternoon. Dad tied her to your swing because she had been chasing the cats and the rope twisted until she suffocated."

I was pastor, undertaker, soloist and mourner at her funeral. After placing a bouquet of pink cosmos on her grave and singing, "Jesus Loves Me," I marked her grave with a shingle and printed "Patsey" on it with white chalk. Our friends, Orville and Marion, had my favorite French poodle named Peppy who lived up to his name. He became so excited when I visited that he raced through the house, from kitchen and hall to living room. He had strong dislikes as well and made no secret of his feelings. Peppy was my all time favorite away from home dog.

My most unfavorite away from home dog was large, black and ill tempered. I biked ten miles selling V.F.W. poppies one Memorial weekend. One look at me and this dog viciously attacked. Mother carefully dressed my leg with peroxide and strips of sheeting. We never thought of rabies.

Tiny, a Pekinese, was my son Doug's dog. They were inseparable for years. Doug was killed in an accident and Tiny, as the rest of our family, was unconsolable. He sat by the door awaiting Doug's return. After a few months, he became terminally ill and we had to tearfully leave him at the vet's.

My friend Ray had a seeing eye dog named Greta. Smart and dedicated to her master, she obeyed his orders and provided safety so he could walk at her side with a steady, easy stride. Greta was playful when out of harness. In harness, she was a professional.

My grandchildren have three beautiful dogs. Their mother, Janis, keeps them well-groomed and healthy. The four children enjoy their pets. They are also excellent watchdogs.

Reminiscing about these dogs makes me aware that something is missing from my life. Be it friend or foe.

NUMBER, PLEASE

You walk into the kitchen to see a light blinking on your answering machine. You are compelled to press the play button before removing your coat or placing your purse on a chair. You scramble for a pencil to list the messages, starring the ones to answer immediately.

As you remove your coat to make coffee, you think how enslaved you have become to the telephone and answering machine. Nary a call escapes you. When you go for a walk or take a nap, it leaves a message; you receive pitches for charities you've never heard of, for money you don't have. However, most calls come from friends and can be returned at your leisure.

You drink your coffee and remember a less complicated life. Downright simple. When your telephone ring was one long and three short. With seven people on your party line, you could lift the receiver and listen (rubberneck) to other conversations.

You remember the operator (Central) always awake, always cheerful, the heartbeat of the community. You can hear her melodious voice saying, "Number, please." You recall the time she located the doctor when you were thrown from a horse. She, the keeper of secrets, counselor of many, a harbinger of the hot line, was dependable. You could depend on her to blow the noon whistle and to ring the fire alarm.

A long distance call meant an emergency such as

Aunt Thelma's car accident. You can't remember a long distance call just to visit. Just for fun.

Your husband remembers a neighbor playing his new phonograph on the party line for all rubbernecks to enjoy. As a little boy, he bumped his head on the telephone shelf so often he developed a blood blister and, fifty years later, is still bald in that spot.

There is a telephone in every room in your house, including the bathroom. When you were a child, there was one telephone in each home, usually located on the wall near the kitchen table.

This telephone was a large oak box resembling a face with no humor, no smile. The mouthpiece its nose, two brass bells for eyes, one ear a ringer, the other a black receiver at the end of a cord. The shelf, its mouth on which you doodled as you talked.

The new telephone would surprise Alexander Graham Bell. He would be shocked at the cellular phone and astonished to see telephones on planes. It would be hard for him to comprehend your ability to monitor an unwelcome call by seeing the caller's phone number and name on your screen.

You realize you are on the threshold of the 21st century and hitherto unknown technology will be developed. Soon you may wear a telephone on your wrist or finger, or an answering machine implanted as a pacemaker under your skin. Your great-great-grandchildren may phone home from a planet in a yet undiscovered solar system.

But for now, you stop recalling the past or dreaming of the future and get to work returning those calls recorded on your answering machine.

FANTASY, PURE AND SIMPLE

What if . . .
You have a phone call from the President
You meet your identical twin
A space ship lands in your front yard
Your husband buys a one-way ticket to Bali
This morning you weigh 120 pounds
There is a kangaroo in your living room
And a giraffe in your kitchen
You receive a check for $453,000
Your hair turns gray overnight
Your hair turns red overnight
Your hair turns black overnight
You forget what you color your hair is
Your doctor promises you will live to 100
Suddenly, overnight, you are 99 years old
Your husband brings you two dozen roses
He brings them everyday—
You are allergic to roses
You discover you are a member of royalty
And that you are thirty years younger
Your mother phones from Heaven
        to correct your grammar
Your book makes the nonfiction best seller list
You are asked to run for Vice-President
You decide to spend the next four years in space,
                        then what . . .

A NEW TWIST ON TIME

You turn on your television and hear a special announcement by the evening news anchor. His usual well-modulated voice tremulous with emotion.

"Ladies and Gentlemen, the most remarkable news of this century is breaking as I speak. Scientists have discovered we will have one more hour in every day starting in the year 2000."

You feel befuddled. It means 365 more hours in a year. What a bonus. It is too good to be true, you think. Impossible.

Two hours later, the President addresses the nation and announces he will call a summit meeting of world leaders to decide how to cope with this astonishing news.

"After which I shall appoint a commission to study the effect of a twenty-five hour day on our national life. This will be a bipartisan group of men and women, co-chaired by leaders from both parties."

You hear him through your mental fog go on to plea for national unity and God's help. You are cognizant that this moment will be programmed into your brain. Forever. The same as it was the day President Kennedy was shot.

You remember the instructor announcing in class, "The President has been shot."'"

You were sitting in the second row from the front and wearing a green and gold jacket and matching slacks. After a collective gasp, the room fell silent.

Following his announcement, the instructor dismissed the class.

The morning after the President's address, *The Republic* carries the text of his speech under a banner headline, PRESIDENT PLEAS FOR UNITY. You eagerly read the additional three pages of speculation about the effects of a nine-hour day. Some columnists speculate on anticipated changes in the stock market and gross national product. Other columnists anticipate physiological and societal adaptations to the hitherto unknown time change.

You are encouraged to send to send your ideas to 2000 TIME HELP.

You wonder about simple things like one more hour before dinner. Will it mean a longer cocktail hour or an additional valuable hour with family?

You wonder if people will age faster, have gray hair at twenty or arthritis at thirty.

You think of the stock market boom in the clock industry. In a digital clock you wonder where they will place the extra hour. If they place it in the morning, the lucky larks will rise an hour early. Whereas if the additional hour is in the evening, the doves will rejoice. Both doves and larks will have no excuse not to write that letter, read that book, start those exercises or clean that drawer.

You expect a twelve and a half hour face on a traditional clock. An extra hour a day means seven extra hours a week. More than three days a month adds up to a staggering thirty-six days a year.

Thinking about stocks and calendars boggles your mind. You decide to stop obsessing and leave it to the world leaders to make their decisions. But, like clockwork, your mind returns again and again to these questions.

Whatever way this hour a day is utilized, you know

you can take the time to become computer literate or you may be able to have a piano lesson every week with an extra hour a day for practice.

What if advanced beings from other planets are already on a twenty-five or thirty hour day? During the next thousand years, man will discover their concept of time and how they spend it.

You are thankful you will never again have to hear that phrase, "I don't have time." Procrastinators will no longer have the excuse of not having enough time. The truth will emerge why they don't accomplish their tasks.

Your mental fog clears as you realize it will be up to each of us, as individuals, to gratefully acknowledge this gift of an extra hour a day in the next millennium.

ON LOOKING BACK

Uncle Carl, dean of women, was surrounded by daughters. Five of them. Girls with bangs, girls with braids, blonde girls, brunette girls.

"All lovely, all smart," he said with no hint of embarrassment over his pride.

Aunt Millie was feminine and smart with the prettiest legs in the choir and she could shoot the first deer of the season.

My cousin Muriel spent several weeks a summer at our farm home. We traveled the gravel road to the farm with Toby harnessed to a two-wheel cart. Toby was a Depression horse. Lean, slow, wrenlike and infinitely patient. We stopped for lunch three times in tree-sheltered areas. Toby shared our peanut butter sandwiches and bananas with apparent relish.

At our last lunch stop, a kindly gray-haired lady came out from her farm house and asked, "Where are you girls going?"

"Rollag," I replied.

"My goodness, you girls had best hurry up because

you have a long, long way to go before you get to Rollag."

We continued, the cart creaking on its two wheels down the dusty road, stopping every few minutes to rest the tired horse.

"Poor Toby," Muriel murmured as she chased mosquitoes off his well-worked back. Toby nuzzled her neck in gratitude.

The sunset was fading as the horse labored over the last hill toward the small white farmhouse with its welcoming yellow light shining from the kitchen window. Fifteen miles in seven hours. Not as fast as Dad's Model A Ford. More human. The Ford didn't pause to nibble a stray bit of brown grass from the middle of the road.

There were hugs and kisses on arrival.

"Didn't the mosquitoes eat you up?" Mother worried.

"No, but poor Toby," Muriel answered, patting Toby's head.

Both Muriel and I were tired and dirty but happy to see my parents. Dad unharnassed Toby and led him to the barn for water, a bucket of oats and a well-deserved rest.

Several years later, my bicycle trip to Barnesville was faster than our trip with the horse and cart. The county fair was in town and I was invited to stay at Aunt Millie's and go to the fair with Muriel. Early in the morning I biked the fifteen miles from our farm.

The small black oilcloth suitcase bounced in my bike basket. I had saved some money and it jangled in my pocket as I pedaled up and down the gravel hills. The trip took a mere forty-five minutes. They were eating breakfast when I came, the dean, his wife and his daughters. But there was room for me at the table.

The fair was enchanting, the lights brilliant in the early evening and the scent of popcorn and hotdogs heavy in the air. All ages, grandparents to babies, roamed the fairgrounds from the horse stables to the 4-H buildings, to the carnival with its hawkers enticing people to enter their sideshow or toss a ring on a peg to get a life-sized baby doll.

We drank a new soda, the newest on the market, and rode that long arm steel creature, the octopus.

Later, staggering from the whirling steel arms, we agreed that the soda didn't live up to its name. It only came up six times.

REMEMBERING REFRIGERATORS

My side-by-side refrigerator, covered with Christmas photos, reminds me of past attempts to safeguard food.

I remember my parents' water cooler, located between the gasoline pump and the livestock watering tank. Perishables were placed in green fruit jars and, as creatures from Outer Space, floated in the water. This cooler was perfect for setting gelatin. Red gelatin with bananas floating on the top.

In the winter months, Mother made wonderful maplenut ice cream, frozen under a dishpan turned upside down in the snow.

My husband and I rented a walk-up two-bedroom apartment after World War II. The Ice Man carried a twenty-pound chunk of ice up the stairway and deposited it in the ice compartment of the oak icebox. When I returned from work, my first task was to empty the overflow pan. On hot days this pan overflowed on the floor.

In a year we moved to an apartment with an electric refrigerator. It was short and squat, its cooling element a gigantic hat on its top.

Three years later we moved to our first house. The refrigerator door was in the kitchen and the rest of the of the appliance built into the garage. A space saver. Its frozen food compartment held five pounds of meat in small packages.

Later, we enlarged our family and our kitchen. The

new appliances were coppertone. The refrigerator had a large freezer with its separate door. Our friend, the milkman, filled it three times a week with quart bottles of milk. We used the cream on the top for our cereal.

My next refrigerator was avocado green and self-defrosting. Its freezer supplemented by an upright freezer. By then, there were only two of us and the refrigerator was bursting with food.

The tales a refrigerator could tell if only it could, and would, talk.

HOPELESSLY LOST

Ibelong to an unfortunate group of people who have no innate sense of direction. Therefore, I am in a perpetual state of being lost.

This getting lost is not amusing, albeit I have been the butt of many a family joke.

I have fired the fuel of their jokes by telling tales on myself.

In one such tale, I parked in front of St. Luke's School of Nursing and after a twelve hour day I started looking for my car. I walked around the block. No gold Nova. Finally, I phoned a friend and we cruised the area.

A light flashed into my dimmed brain.

"I think I parked in a 'No Parking Zone'."

We drove to the police station and found I had been issued a ticket every hour. After ten tickets the car was impounded.

The next day I paid the $75 fee and rescued my car from its jail.

I have been lost in Cormorant. Cormorant isn't exactly Chicago. My cousin, who gets lost as easily as I, heard there was a new business in Cormorant so we went exploring and walked into someone's house by mistake. We backed out the door and burst into hysterical laughter. Inadvertently, we had made history. We had become lost in Cormorant.

Sunland Village in Mesa, Arizona isn't Chicago either. Soon after I moved to this mile square retirement community, I went for a Sunday afternoon walk. After admiring gardenia and hibiscus bushes as well as cactus for an hour, I decided to return home.

I became hopelessly lost.

It took directions from four friendly folks before I found my way home. In subsequent walks that winter, I carried a map of the Village in my pocket.

Eight years later, I no longer need a map but keep the same route and follow street signs.

Because it is so difficult for me to find my way, I allow myself an extra half hour before an appointment. It keeps me punctual. If early, I spend the extra time reading or resting in my car.

The first winter in Mesa, I taped a hand-drawn map of the major streets to my dash. Now they are memorized but when travelling in Scottsdale or Phoenix, up goes another map.

I have often wondered why directions come easily to some and not for others. My husband says, "Just look at the sun. Remember it always rises in the east and sets in the west." In the "Valley of the Sun," he thinks this is easy. It sounds simple (so does the Theory of Relativity). But I can't lean out my car window to look for the sun without getting a fender bender or a sunburn.

My parents taught me directions from their front porch which faced north. To my right was east, to my left, west and behind me, south. Easy.

Decades later, it takes time and energy to place myself in that front porch.

My front porch faces east. This really complicates things.

COMPANY COMING

I love company. Often. Many guests. But something invariably goes wrong.

I smell rubber burning and the vacuum cleaner stops. It takes time to retrieve the quarter from its innards and I have no spare vacuum belt. The garbage disposal becomes plugged with carrot peelings. The toilet doesn't flush.

If the guests are to spend the weekend, everything happens at once; no repairmen work on weekends.

Our guests were due to arrive in an hour and my husband poured dishwashing detergent into the dishwasher. Catastrophic suds billowed over the kitchen floor threatening to invade the living room.

We used every towel and blanket in the house (with the exception of the guest towels) to wipe the suds from the floor. The towels and blankets became so heavy with water, Bill took them to the laundry because our washer would have broken under the load.

I shut the dishwasher door on the rest of the suds and we ordered in pizza.

Monday I reran the dishwasher and endured mountains of suds flowing from every crevice in the machine. The repairman suggested vinegar. It didn't work. A friend suggested soda. It didn't work. I worked — running the machine all day for six days until the water ran clear.

"Don't run the dishwasher again," I warned Bill.

"I get the message."

"No matter what, this is the second time you have used the wrong soap. The third time both the dishwasher and I walk."

I had no spark of humor left. He chuckled, secure in my love, knowing I wouldn't leave him over anything as innocuous as a dishwasher.

I, too, have my foibles. Instead of staying home in the kitchen, I take our guests antiquing. After collecting a sample of the ancient wonders of the world, I come home to a three-pound beef roast, raw in the refrigerator. I rub it with herbs and place it into the modern wonder of the kitchen, the microwave. I turn on full power as if I am driving a steam engine up a high grade.

Soon the aroma of roast beef filled the kitchen. We sat down to eat this roast which had turned to stone. My wonderful husband chuckled over my faux pas and brought in pizza.

Recently I invited six girlfriends for lunch. This coincided with a storm leaving our cottage without electricity, telephone or water.

My friends came. We went shopping in Detroit Lakes and had an excellent lunch at a restaurant. It was far better than I was planning at home. Not pizza.

I wonder if I have a subliminal dislike for company, for it seems strange to have so many problems when entertaining guests.

I think I'll encourage drop-in company, as my parents had on their farm, during the thirties. If no one dropped in by three on a Sunday afternoon, we bundled into the car to visit the neighbors. I'll roll back the years to a simple, less stressful life. I'll just learn to make potato salad and red gelatin every Sunday. Then wait.

Yes, I love company. Our guests may expect something unpredictable. Then predictably, we will have pizza.

MITSY, THE CLOWN

I have a red and yellow clown suit. With a necktie. And suspenders. When I put it on, I become a new person. A person with a vivid personality all her own.

My name changes to Mitsy.

My first clowning experience was at a church clown workshop where I learned basic clowning principles:

- Never make a fool of someone other than yourself or another clown.
- Make a fool of yourself. You are no longer you.
- A clown is always a clown.
- Clowns have no voice and they must "show" the world what is important.
- Everyone has a message.

The talented clown conducting the workshop helped us change our appearance with makeup. We dressed in lively, mismatched clothes and visited residents of a nearby nursing home. Having worked as a nurse for more than thirty years, it was strange to have reactions to Mitsy, the clown.

It was as bringing sunshine into a dark room. Bored faces lit with surprise and pleasure. All but one resident.

One look at Mitsy and she covered her eyes and screamed.

Ten years later I attended another workshop in Tucson, Ariz. to learn additional techniques of clown art, preparatory to a performance at a convention of Women of the ELCA. There were six of us would-be clowns.

We practiced expressions of happiness, sadness, anger, fear and terror and learned to pantomime. We opened invisible doors, juggled invisible balls and preened before invisible mirrors. We practiced using small props such as whistles, scarves and balloons.

We spent hours learning to apply clown makeup and received individual help from our instructor. No face resembled another but we were all clowns.

Two months later we performed in Phoenix at a dinner for three hundred women. An hour before performance we gathered in a large dressing room to assume a new persona. We laughed as we awkwardly dressed in our flamboyant clown suits. My flowered red and yellow suit had pockets deep enough for all my props. I tucked in a bag of candy kisses to throw to the women.

We put on our white faces, the white face a symbol of death to self.

I felt strange applying the thick white makeup to my entire face, covering eyebrows and lips. I drew green eyebrows, arched high over my eyes. I placed an enormous red mouth, smiling "ear to ear," and placed high spots of red color high on my cheekbones.

Next, I glued into place a red plastic button nose. My face was topped by a curly green wig and an enormous red flowered bow.

I smiled at Mitsy in the mirror.

A few minutes of additional pantomime practice followed by relaxation exercises and we were ready to perform.

Because a clown never talks, only pantomimes, I

was tired after the hour but enjoyed the experience. This time no one screamed.

Mitsy has come out of her closet several times since this performance. Each time we become better acquainted.

She is one happy but exhausting clown.

WONDERLAND

The first snowfall
blankets trees and grasses
with diamond studded white fluff.
Moist snow sifts
into my summer sandals
melting beneath my toes.
Enthralled by the first snowfall,
I catch a snowflake
on my tongue
and dance into a wonderland.

THE SHADOWBOXES

Daddy, I dreamed about you last night. You, such a stern disciplinarian, were warm and caring in my dream. You photographed me in front of giant shadowboxes.

Belatedly, I recognize I was the center of your life. You wanted the background just right and took so many pictures which you carefully developed in your darkroom.

As I am nearing the age you were when you died, a shadow of your former self hollowed by strokes, I accept the legacy you left me. A legacy of honor, responsbility and humor. A legacy of love.

We will never be able to explore together the shadowboxes of last night's dream; however, I feel the warmth and caring you had such difficulty verbalizing when I was a child.

Instead, you made me the central figure in all your snapshots.

ANOTHER LITTLE MERMAID

It is possible my husband is the only man alive to sleep with a nude painting of his wife's aunt hanging above his bed.

She was my special occasion aunt. The glamorous one who lived across the country in large cities. Baltimore, Chicago, and San Francisco.

Aunt Dora came for weddings and was as beautiful as the bride. She came for funerals and was the center of attention at the post-funeral luncheon in the church basement. She wore designer clothes on her fabulous figure. Her tiny feet were encased in exquisite imported shoes. She was the mistress of the oneliners.

Dora didn't attend high school or college as did her three sisters who became rural schoolteachers. Or attend the university and become a professor as did her brother.

She was labeled at ten years of age as "the weak one."

"You must watch over her, she is not strong," the county school nurse advised her mother.

That same mother, whose son had died only the year before from peritonitis, heeded this advice and Dora became imprisoned by her alleged weakness.

The year was 1932, a drab Depression year. Dora, restless and lonesome, subscribed to a lonely hearts magazine. Walking through the dusty grasses to the mailbox, she hid it in her blouse so her mother wouldn't see it.

She read Paul's description. He read hers. They corresponded two years. She, an unsophisticated twenty-year-old farm girl. He, twenty years her senior, a graduate from Heidelberg University, had emigrated from an unsettled Germany.

Dora's mother had immigrated to America from Norway as an eighteen-year-old, eager to escape her own strict and humorless mother. And now it was Dora who, over protestations by her mother, boarded the train to Chicago to meet her love.

One week later Paul and Dora married.

Soon after, he painted a nude picture of her, modeled after Denmark's Little Mermaid.

For sixty years this watercolor hung over my aunt's bed as my weak aunt lived until her heart failed at the age of 92.

Since her death, this painting has hung above our bed. I find it strange that visitors never comment on the painting for it is a fine painting.

Perhaps they think the picture is of me. I hope so.

READING FOR THE MINISTER

We called confirmation class "reading for the minister." For two summers, sixteen of us gathered at 10 a.m every Monday morning at Rollag Church to study Luther's Small Catechism. We sat on the left side of the aisle in front of the piano. I volunteered to play "God's Word is Our Inheritance" for our opening hymn. I knew the notes for the right hand and the left hand followed along.

Reverend Hauge taught the class. He had short gray hair and a brooding expression on his broad Norwegian face. Brooding until he smiled—then his face lit with an incandescent glow.

I was mesmerized by his shoes. They were enormous. I mentally measured them as he stood in front of us. He walked slowly, toeing out. I thought if he walked toes ahead, like the rest of us, he would trip over his own feet.

Pastor taught by telling stories to illustrate a point, much as another teacher taught by parables nearly two thousand years ago. He made biblical characters come alive. They were human, like us.

After class, we biked a mile to my aunt's house and went swimming in a muddy and bloodsucker-infested slough.

My aunt always served us lunch. Orange nectar and cookies. Truly, confirmation class was a highlight of my young life. As was my aunt's hospitality.

THE ROCKER

I sit in my antique rocker and listen to its story. In the eye of my mind I see a baby in a long white dress. In the ear of my mind I hear a soft lullaby as she sleeps in this golden oak rocker, this sleeping baby who will become my grandmother.

I cuddle my doll on the gliders' soft cushion while my grandma makes lingonberry crepes for our breakfast.

Soon the rocker becomes Mother's and I rock four boy babies. A fourth generation to fall asleep in this manner.

After my grandson is born, Mother gives me the rocker. The first of the fifth generation lulled asleep by its magic.

Now, this age old rocker waits quietly in my living room for a splendid new home and the rest of its story.

HOOKED ON MAKEUP

As a teenager, I fantasied I just might become beautiful if I wore the right makeup. My first purchase, at age 13, was a 25-cent Tangee lipstick which changed from colorless in the tube to a soft pink on my lips. I felt it created a dramatic change in my appearance.

An even more dramatic change occurred a few years later when I applied Max Factor's pancake makeup. I used a damp sponge to even out the application but my neck was decidedly whiter than my face. Mother brought considerable pressure on me to abandon Max because she said it left cracks in my smile.

Our hired girl introduced me to eyebrow makeup. She was a redhead and it looked great on her but my brows were black and I couldn't notice any change in my appearance when I wore it. But I loved the narrow red box with its tiny mirror and delicate brush.

My fascination with cosmetics endures. I have a shelf filled with free gifts because each time a bonus is offered with a cosmetic order, I succumb to my addiction.

As I try yet another exotic eyeshadow, I hope to find the magic potion where, on application, I will become a beauty.

Until then, I remain hooked on makeup.

CRAZY FOR DENIM

Sixty years ago I wouldn't have been caught out of the barn dressed in denim. Or, for that matter, in the barn dressed in denim. For denim was restricted to mattress material or men's work clothes, such as the striped and shapeless overalls supported by heavy crisscrossed suspenders hanging from the shoulder. Another option, dark blue heavy-weight denim, held at the waist by a leather belt. These were worn by farm boys for field work but they were never worn by farm girls.

We girls wore slacks. Not to school, just at home and for recreation. These slacks were made of soft cotton, wool or "sharkskin" and had matching tops. Butcher tops we called them.

Then things changed. Our sons sported denims renamed "jeans". They came in gray and green beside the traditional blue. They were reinforced at the knees.

My eldest son wore his left knee through the reinforcement before the second washing. Finally, after patching the outside, I learned to iron on a patch underneath the left reinforced knee. It was thick and puckered, but it worked.

Both middle sons wore their knees evenly. With each washing, the knee area just became more faded. Finally both knees wore through about the time the jeans were too tight and short. Highwater jeans, we called them.

Then came my youngest son. This gentle giant never wore a hole in either knee because he grew so fast he had new jeans before the old ones wore out.

My jeans clothes wash was impressive. Four pair of jeans for each boy, sixteen jeans side by side on the clothes line. I hung them by the legs or the waist, whichever came first out of the basket. The clothes lines looked like a staff of musical notes.

My grandchildren don't get holes in their jeans either. They wear them three sizes too large and hold them in place with suspenders. Most overalls are so loose the body doesn't touch the fabric, therefore they last. Forever. There is no fear of heavy patches on stovepipe jeans and no brass rivets to scratch their skin.

My generation, the grandparent one, has discovered the wearability and versatility of blue denim. The new look. I own a denim wardrobe, including a denim hat. It is soft and comfortable with its high crown and narrow brim. It has a puffy, frazzled look. As much at home in the Southwest as the Northland.

But best of all are my denim colored suede shoes. A friend and I own identical denim outfits and we frequently make plans to wear them at the same time. She hasn't washed hers yet and it looks fresh and new.

Unlike a farmer I knew long ago who never washed his overalls. They were covered with grease and smelled of the fruits of the barn. He wore them to town on errands. When they rotted, full of dirt, he discarded them for a new pair. All this changed the day he married. From that day forward he wore clean overalls. This demonstrates the power of a woman.

I can envision the first presidential ball in the new millennium. Many women will wear diamond studded denim with long denim skirts sweeping the floor.

I find it unbelievable, well nigh impossible, for a Rollag farm girl, born in the twenties, to own a wardrobe of denim.

In the ear of my mind, I hear my shocked father telling my mother when he sees his daughter dressed in denim, "Can you imagine Angela, at her age, crazy for denim?"

A PENNY, A NICKEL, AND A DIME

As a child in the thirties, a penny was important to me. Penny candy was abundant. My favorite candy was a cellophane wrapped roll of discs each marked a penny, a nickel or a dime. Great play money.

I spent endless hours making change to my imaginary customers after serving them lemonade from my orange crate stand in our front yard. Then I drank the lemonade.

I begged Mother to allow me to take my lemonade stand to the end of our driveway and sell to real instead of imaginary customers. I planned to charge three cents a glass and expected a large crowd because our farm was located off the "lake road."

Her answer was an unequivocal "No." When I started to cry, she went on to explain, "In the first place, they won't stop and you might get run over for those cars are speeding. Why, they go 35-45 miles per hour!"

That same year Dad paid his hired man twenty dollars a month with board and room and Sundays off. I gave the hired man free lemonade from my stand. Sometimes he reciprocated by taking my sister and me to the movies.

My first paying job was for my father who hired me as a milkmaid for three cents a cow if I milked her both morning and evening. I milked three cows and had Sunday off, receiving fifty-four cents a week. I enjoyed my job because Dad and I sang as we milked the cows.

"Oh, Suzannah" was his favorite.

This job had its occupational hazards. A cow's tail and legs were unpredictable. She switched her tail at the flies on her back and, although I was adept at dodging, often the slimy tail landed on my face, providing a rich brown color on my cheeks.

I experimented, thinking if I placed the stool between two cows and milked the first one on the right and turned and milked the second one on the left, it would be more efficient. A cow is a creature of habit; therefore, seconds later I picked myself up from the other side of the barn.

It was my responsibility to keep books on my milking operation. I saved two dollars and sixteen cents a month and in two years bought my first piano.

Mother told stories of teaching rural school for fifteen dollars a month and room and board. The wonderful folks with whom she stayed became lifelong friends.

We also boarded the teacher. I'm not sure about her salary but I know we as a family enjoyed her. Dishes were done expediently with Mother washing and teacher and me wiping. Confidences were shared over the dishwater and Mother and my teacher forged a friendship which was to last until she brought roses from her garden to the hospital the day Mother died.

I was careful when I spent a nickel. I once spent one on a high mound of peanut candy with a cherry flavored center. It tasted different. Weird. Horrified, I saw a half worm on the peanuts. This candy bar had passed its shelf life and I nearly passed out, not knowing if I had swallowed the other half of the worm.

A dime was alot of money. It was enough to buy my father a long and black Cuban cigar. My Mother didn't appreciate this because the smell permeated our living room and car.

This car was a maroon Whippet with a lovely burl dashboard. A nickel, dime and penny bought a gallon of gas. Dad was the Whippet's second owner and I found a treasure under the rear plush seat. It was a chunk of petrified wood which weighed two pounds. My parents concluded that the car had been driven to the Petrified Forest in Arizona.

My cousin and I frequently purchased a double headed ice cream cone for a dime. We could enjoy three flavors on a cone if the third scoop didn't drop off. It was enough to spoil our supper. But delicious.

My husband still stoops to pick up a penny he finds on the sidewalk. For a penny, a nickel and a dime are still legal tender. Even more, they evoke priceless memories.

ALL OR NOTHING AT ALL

You are very young when first you notice the "All or Nothing" syndrome. This knowledge is reinforced by events all your life.

It is either good fortune or bad. Some folks blame a full moon or a cosmic roll. Others contribute it to luck or a fortune cookie. But all agree good and bad events tend to cluster.

The telephone is a classic example of the all or nothing syndrome, some days only telemarketers—other days friends and family convey warm messages and you respond in kind.

If you are single, you go for months without a phone call from a significant male. Suddenly, the phone vibrates with eligible men vying for your time.

This feast or famine syndrome plays out during your career. For years, you stagnate at a job with no possibility of promotion. Suddenly, more than one position opens with new salary schedules and a possibility of promotion or transfer.

You go shopping for a new summer wardrobe. One day nothing fits. The colors are not attractive. You try on seven dresses and nothing looks like it belongs on you. Less than a week later, you shop in the same stores and four outfits are stunning. Made for you. Now you must choose.

Somedays you try on every outfit you own before one seems even half right for the occasion. Other days, everything looks great and you dress in ten minutes.

Except for shoes. You own more than the two you had when you were ten. More than twenty pair, collected over the years, clutter your closet. You have the right shoes for the right occasion, except the present one — no navy pumps.

Even the weather clusters with its good and bad days. Rotten weather makes you a prisoner in your own home. Then the sun comes from behind a cloud, the flowers bloom and all of nature welcomes you, sparking your energies, your interests and your intellect.

You browse the library. Books center on the topics of your interest. Other days, nary a one is worth reading.

Your friends. Same people, different days. Somedays they are open and friendly, other days they are closed, their eyes glazing over as you speak.

If you are married, your husband vacillates between supportive tenderness and . . .

What about you? Do you arise early and eager for days, weeks, and months before hitting the downer days?

Some evenings there are great TV programs, so many you record several for future viewing. Other evenings, nothing.

You search for evidence of the scientific meaning to this all or nothing syndrome. As you ponder with your pencil, the doorbell rings. It is your next door neighbor.

"I just baked some sugar cookies and brought you a dozen."

"Sit down, I'll put on the coffee."

You notice the sun is shining and the flowers are blooming.

THE PICTURE AND I

I knew why she came. I had known for months that she would come. In my early waking hours and in my day-dreams, I could see her coming. Carrying the picture. The ugly picture, soon to become mine.

I thought, *I'll never tell a lie again, even a kind white lie.*

It all began thirty years ago. My friend, Elaine, bought the picture of her dreams and hung it above the beige sofa in her modest living room. Her family teased her constantly about the picture. No one liked it. Except Elaine.

The picture was painted in shades of beige as hard to understand as a foreign language known only to the artist and Elaine. If you used your imagination you could see two pillars, one on each side of the picture. If you pulled a little string with a beige wooden head attached, two tiny lights appeared on top of those two pillars.

When I first saw the picture, Elaine was in tears.

"No one likes it," she said.

I pulled on the string and said, "Let there be light," and there was light. We both laughed and the picture began to have a life of its own.

The furniture in the room changed with the years but the picture remained in the same place.

A constant.

Elaine's daughter, Anita, married and moved out to establish her own home. The grandchildren came to visit. Each, in turn, pulled the string and the lights continued to appear atop the towers in the picture.

Elaine's husband, Urban, died. The lights still lit.

Then she became ill. She was told the cancer was incurable. She rested hours each day on a new beige sofa under that same beige picture.

When I saw her, emaciated and weak, I smiled as when I had first seen the picture and turned on its lights. We laughed, we cried, and talked of many things under that dim light.

Each week I came to visit. Always I turned on the light when I came and off when I left. It became a ritual.

Soon the picture with its light was alone in the room.

Anita smiled as she reached into her trunk and removed the picture, its frayed cord limp at its side.

"I brought you a remembrance from Mother. She said you always had loved this picture."

THANKSGIVING MEMORIES

A certain magic occurs each Thanksgiving Day. Ungratefulness changes to thankfulness, selfishness becomes unselfishness, goodness overcomes evil, and so on . . .

For Thanksgiving is a holiday and we expect good things. What we expect, we get. A national self-fulfilling prophesy. The national news becomes softer and the TV anchors more gentle. We see pictures of homeless eating turkey and pumpkin pie. Just like you and me.

The elderly, without families nearby, crowd into large auditoriums with caterers providing turkey and trimmings.

This year we Brady snowbirds gather at our home in Mesa, Arizona. My husband's brother and wife, his sister and her husband, another sister and us. That same Brady bunch who attended Thanksgiving Eve Service at St. Peter Lutheran. A joyous, thankfilled service where sacks of food were gathered for the homeless and needy of Mesa.

We spent nearly two hours at the table.

This is the year I placed Mother's lovely hand-crocheted tablecloth and set it with the blue and white china she gave me when she moved to Bethany Towers in Fargo.

I made the selfsame dinner that she used to make, without the homemade buns. But it didn't taste the same. It missed its mark. Perhaps because my eyes were too misty with memories. Only the mashed potatoes and gravy tasted the same.

My husband tells of taking his son and daughter for a long walk through the woods near Belleville, Illinois each Thanksgiving morning to pick bittersweet for the Thanksgiving dinner table, while his wife stayed home to tend the turkey. One year their dinner was four hours late; a power company employee had too much Thanksgiving cheer and pushed over a power pole in their backyard. A half-done turkey had to wait until the power came on.

I shared the story of Eatmore, the turkey. One of several hundred turkeys in my family's flock. Eatmore was one of the turkeys who flew to Mother's shoulders when she poured the turkey mash in their feeder. One morning his foot was broken, somehow he had caught it in a trap. He became the turkey for our feast and all twenty-seven pounds of him filled the roaster. They told me he was juicy and succulent, but Mother and I didn't eat a morsel of turkey that year.

Perhaps we were too busy to eat. I helped Mother serve over twenty-five guests for dinner that Thanksgiving. Grandmas, aunts, uncles, cousins in addition to our family of four. The dinner was traditional, crusty candied sweet potatoes and wonderful scalloped corn. I sneaked a few extra spoonsful after dinner when it was cooling on the pantry shelf.

The meal included homemade buns, dill and sweet pickles, cranberry relish and beet pickles. Pumpkin pie, made with cream and just the right spices, was served with homemade vanilla ice cream, which Dad, my uncle, cousins and I helped to freeze.

After dinner men and women congregated into different rooms. Recipes and politics didn't mix. We children played in the barn and my oldest cousin told stories, great plots but we had to supply our own endings.

It was a wonderful day for everyone except Eatmore.

LIFTING OFF FOR HOME

The plane lifts away from the city
with its little houses
and grand structures.
Silver wings span the sky
and reflect the sun.
The humming engines
sing of home.

A HOLE IN ONE

I see the golf ball in my dreams. The ball rolls across the green and eases into the cup. The ball arches high in the air and plays into the cup. The ball curves gently down the fairway, rolls over the green, into the cup. Three holes in one, but only in my dreams.

My first memories of golf are from an encyclopedia in a one-room country school. Our eighth grade teacher assigned us an essay on an individual sport. There were five students in my grade. Tennis, skiing, bowling and swimming were all chosen.

With trepidation, I asked, "Golf?"

"Fine," she replied, and I began my research.

The red encyclopedia covered the game of golf in a several page article, accompanied by pictures. I read that fairways were grass and greens were sand. I learned there were woods, irons and putters. I found the purpose of the game was to putt a small ball into a round hole in the green.

Easy, I thought. *Silly,* I thought.

My next experience was more than twenty years later when, as an older-than-average college student, I played golf in physical education. I found out it wasn't easy and it wasn't silly. It was hard work. I constantly whiffed the ball.

I was embarrassed because the rest of my class was younger and most of them had played golf. Their balls sailed down the fairway. The instructor called my golf swing flat and took extra time with me, to no avail. My swing was identical to my softball swing. My "C" grade was a gift for I deserved to fail.

I fell in love with Bill and golf at the same time. We went golfing every day of our courtship. Bill was, and is, a golf addict. He hits a long and straight ball. He gave me golf lessons for my birthday.

"Ah, ha," the instructor said, "I see you have played softball."

My friendly foursome gathers each Tuesday and Thursday in our woman's league. The three hit a hard and long ball. They are low handicappers.

They inspire me and I walk up to my ball. I hit it ten feet down the fairway. No mulligans on ladies' day. I choose another club and walk toward the ball. I could have gone further if I had closed my eyes. The third connects with the ball and I surprise myself. I hear cheers from the group as the ball flies down the fairway. The fourth ball and I am on the fringe of the green. A chip catapults the ball three feet from the pin.

I study the terrain like a pro and draw my putter slowly back and push it forward. The ball misses the cup by a hair and rolls two feet behind it. A lucky putt brings my score to seven. A seven is not a lucky number in golf.

Undaunted, I continue the round of golf. A short hole, a mere 86 yards. I choose my club as carefully as if I were placing an arrow in my bow and walk confidently to the T box. I take a long, slow swing. Follow through, I tell myself. The ball lands on the green, four feet from the cup. I putt softly, taking my time. Two putts and I have a par. The rest of my foursome pars, except for one who has a birdie.

My husband and my friends have had holes in one; therefore, I tell myself, My time will come.

Besides, what difference does it make if I never have a hole in one. How lucky I am. How blessed. A senior strong enough to golf, not house, bed or chair bound. Not yet. Each day a bonus.

Last night my hole in one dream was so realistic, I walked to the pro shop to see if one was posted for me. These golfing dreams are so pleasant that, if I awaken, I try to go to sleep and dream again of another hole in one. I am confident that someday my dream will become reality.

A CHRISTMAS LETTER

Dearest God,

Today is Christmas Day and it is as fresh and new as the first Christmas I can remember. I awoke at sunrise to see the lavender streaks intermingled with the gold and gray of the sky.

It was then I decided to write and thank you for sending us your only son nearly 2,000 years ago. I am grateful for this, your greatest gift of love, for I could never have given even one of my four sons.

One of these sons entered your kingdom early. It comforts me to know someday he will greet me and together we will worship you, our Triune God.

Thank you, God of Christmas.   Love,

Angie

THOUGHTS OF NEW YEAR'S

A new year, that glittering renewal every 365 days. You celebrate between football and dinner. New Year's Day, like all holidays, centers around the dinner table.

You remember New Year's Eve when you were very young. A child. A child who dressed in her mother's discarded dress, its hemline hitting the floor in front of your brown oxfords. You drape a lace curtain over your shoulders pretending it is an evening shawl.

It is Wayne King's music on the radio. Waltz time. Your parents sleep after the ten o'clock news, but you stay up until the mantle clock on the buffet strikes midnight. You fantasize as you move to the music with your imaginary partners.

In your long life you have both attended and given New Year's Eve parties. You have attended New Year's Eve church services. All are pleasant memories.

But this New Year's Day you remember those little girl fantasies with that secret smile you reserve for those long ago memories.

You've given up New Year's resolutions after umpteen years of making a list of at least ten altruistic and well nigh (for you) impossible items: such as reading the Bible through in '42, '52 or '62 . . . or losing twenty pounds—or thirty. Most of your resolutions were badly bent in ten days and broken, downright shattered, by thirty. Afterwards, each bite of ice cream reinforces your guilt.

A spanking new year, no matter that you are a golden age and holding. Within the twelve sheets of your new calendar lie intrigue, mystery and adventure to be discovered and savoured.

Your dimming eyesight sees more. You are cognizant life truly does run faster, but the joy of a sunrise/sunset, the blue heron on the beach, or your grandson fishing off the dock, take on a new dimension.

Your ears no longer are fine tuned but the ear of your appreciation becomes sharper. You appreciate fine music as you never did in the boo boop days of your teens.

Your lose old friends from death or distance, but their memory sustains and supports you, even as illness may hit home in your own older, compromised body.

New friends are made. No matter they are younger or older. No matter you haven't yet history with them. You sense a history of the heart as you share experiences.

Surprisingly, your children develop gray hair while yours, with help, remains unchanged.

You continue to joyfully ride your bike. It is a one-speed on the street of a retirement village. But you still experience joy of cycling, same as when you were fourteen or forty.

You notice you have begun to fantasize in three-dimension. Past, present and future. Childlike, you wonder what you will do with the rest of your life.

You idly page through your new calendar until you reach the perfect month of May, a month of renewal. You anticipate a fantastic summer. You face it with trust as you think, the party isn't over yet.

You are aware of many who feel New Year's Eve and New Year's Day are anticlimactic, too soon after Christmas with its glamour and pageantry. Just another day. But to you it remains an exciting day.

You stop daydreaming and start working. You take

down Christmas decorations and shuffle through the Christmas cards for the last time, writing down the new addresses and rereading the treasured notes. You dismantle the Christmas tree, carefully wrapping each ornament in tissue. You unwind the strings of multi-colored lights, leaving the tree bare, its needles dry and sharp on your fingers. Carefully, you toss it into a nearby snowbank. Later. you hang suet and birdseed on its sheltering branches, food for your winged visitors.

Your work finished, your fantasies stilled, you pour yourself a well-deserved cup of coffee and eat the last of the Christmas cookies.

UNFORGETTABLE

"You are a cute little devil and right on the level." It was a downright disappointing valentine from my first boyfriend. Unforgettable.

My friend only dimly remembers the romantic card she received from her first boyfriend that same year. She does remember it had a beautiful, soulful verse. Forgettable.

I remember childhood valentines housed in a large white box trimmed with red hearts. Before they were delivered to our desks on Valentine's Day, I thought, *Perhaps there are no valentines for me.* Valentines were an indication of popularity; therefore, I never counted them until I came home from school. I was fearful the other girls may have twice as many as I.

One year I carried my stash of valentines home on a windy day. Skiing down a long hill, I dropped them and watched in horror as they, like the tail of a kite, twirled upward and outward. The red hearts were scattered over a wide area of snow covered prairie. They were unrecoverable. My tears froze on my eyelashes before I reached home and Mother's comfort.

Throughout the years I've received many valentines from each of my four sons. Some, my favorites, were homemade with too much white paste on well-thumbed red construction paper.

The verses were a variation of "Roses are red ... I love you, Mom" in lopsided printing. I proudly displayed them until March and then stashed them safely away. This safest of all places remains forever hidden as I don't have even one of those valentines. This haunts me on my "I wish I had been a better mother days."

Years later, two of my sons gave me identical cards. "I picked it for the verse, Mom," each said. These beautiful cards must be in that same safe haven.

I walk by the valentine counter in the card shop hunting for a perfect verse to express my undying love for my husband. After a long search, I am mesmerized by just one card. "Tomorrow," it says, "I'd marry you all over again, Happy Valentine's Day." A world of feeling in these ten words I could have written. But didn't.

Once in a very long while my husband forgets it is Valentine's Day until 4 o'clock in the afternoon when he disappears for an hour and comes home with a giant-sized pink envelope.

He chuckles, "I almost forgot," as he hands me the card. It is the most beautiful "wife" card I have ever seen. Unforgettable.

I reach into my desk to retrieve the valentine of the half hour search. The perfect card.

After a kiss, Bill says, "Let's go out for dinner—your choice." I dress in my valentine best and we eat in my favorite restaurant. The one with the succulent steaks and the raspberry cream cheesecake.

We eat slowly, by candlelight.

Only rarely have I received a box of candy for Valentine's Day. My latest well-publicized diet is guaranteed to discourage chocolates.

Next year I'll buy Bill a large box of chocolates. I'll expect him to share. That would be unforgettable.

COMFORT

Dear Heavenly Father,
Some lives more pristine be
and orderly by far
may I covet not their peace
secure in your comfort.

THE POWER OF COLOR

When I was young I took color for granted. Now that I am no longer young, I see color cascading everywhere. Vibrant color. I see it in my thoughts and dreams and even in my prayers. No matter my vision is dim. No matter I've seen these hues, yea, these many years. Blind friends tell me they see color vividly in their imaginations, in their thoughts and in their dreams.

I can hear color. Color talks. The purple pageantry of royalty echoes in march music. Shades of gray whisper in the early morning fog. An orange stop sign screams stop.

Green is the color of life. The color of shade trees and rain forests, it regulates life on earth. It is a meaning-filled color to farmers who plant seeds and leave the growth to God.

On the other hand, green can be the green of the inexperienced or the green of envy. Green, the color of currency.

From the blue of the distant hills, "from whence cometh my help," to the blue sky reflected in lakes and streams; it is everyman's favorite color.

"True blue" spells honesty, integrity and loyalty. Yet you and I call it "blues" when we become sad or lonely. Blue walls are supposed to tranquilize—they even suppress appetites in dining areas. A poor choice for party rooms as blue causes people to relax, rather than interact with each other. We listen to the haunting music of the blues.

Red, the most lively of all colors, stimulates our nervous system and makes us feel energetic. It is often used in restaurants because it stimulates the appetite. A dash of red livens a room as well as fabric. Red nail polish and lipstick enlivens a woman. Red symbolizes courage and is the most prominent color in flags of most countries.

But red can be the cold of violence—spilt blood and terror. People see red when angry. When finances are "in the red," one is in financial trouble. A red light means stop. The red light districts symbolize prostitution.

Pink, a cousin of red, is insipid by comparison. It is, however, the color of romance. "In the pink," an expression of good health as indicated by well-nourished pink skin. Pink, the color of babies with their pink cheeks and heels. An affectionate color.

Brown, with its beige and taupe down-to-earth derivatives, is a neutral bridge color. We use it often in home decorating. It is easy on the eye. Basic brown. But the brown of burnt grasses symbolizes poverty and malnutrition. Brown smog smothers a bustling city.

If I wear black, I feel ten pounds thinner. But black also is the color of mourning. It can be both drab and sophisticated.

White complements all color. A wardrobe staple for many. A cool color on a hot day. We think of angels, heaven and purity as this pristine color.

Yes, color is truly the essence of life. Birds, fish, animals and especially humans are attracted to color.

BY INVITATION ONLY

It was summer vacation and I was seventeen and bored so I persuaded Mother to let me make toffee.

I had never eaten toffee but had read of toffee pulls and thought it was something my six-year-old sister Marie and I could do together.

Marie measured the sugar, corn syrup, cornstarch, salt and water and we boiled it until a teaspoon of it formed a hard ball when dropped into cold water.

After the candy was cool, we buttered our hands and began to pull. It wasn't as easy as I had thought. Nor as much fun. The glob in my hands felt as alien as sculpture's clay. Marie wasas puzzled as I. Mother, noticing our predicament, washed her hands and joined us.

The three of us pulled the toffee into a lopsided triangle.

A tiny winged creature flew over the candy. I shook my head to chase it away but he considered this an invitation to enter my left ear. Tormented, I danced around the room. The bug beat a devil's dance on my eardrum.

I washed my hands free of toffee and tried to shake out the bug. Nothing worked. Not even my crying and screaming scared him out of my ear.

Mother poured warm oil into my ear. This slowly dripped out, but no insect. It kept beating the drum. My eardrum.

Dad, a small, thin plier in his hand, offered to help.

"No," I thundered. I had seen him use pliers and

knew his persistence.

Marie watched in shocked silence.

"I'm driving to Barnesville to see the doctor."

The bug and I began the fifteen-mile drive to town. It was a drum-beating drive.

Dr. Simison put a bright light over his eye and took an instrument (I shut my eyes) and put it into my ear.

The walls and ceiling moved uncertainly around me for what seemed hours, in reality only a few minutes.

"Here he is."

A speck of a bug lay on the dressing. Dead.

I sat for half an hour in the waiting room until I recovered my equilibrium, then drove home.

Dad met me at the door.

"How did it go?"

"Fine, nothing to it."

Mother and Marie had finished pulling the toffee but somehow it had lost its appeal.

WHATEVER HAPPENED TO . . .

Cream and Bread:

Something is missing from my life. A special food like cream and bread, the staple of my childhood.

Mother's luscious homemade white bread sliced thicker at one end than the other and laden with heavy cream, crowned with chokecherry jelly or a generous sprinkle of brown sugar, was a mouthwatering delight.

Dad cut his portion into perfect squares and twirled these squares with his fork into the little pool of cream which oozed onto the plate from the cream soaked bread.

One summer day our pastor dropped in.

"Don't fuss, Selma. I'll be happy with cream and bread."

Cream and bread! She was insulted because she enjoyed a reputation as an excellent cook. He ate chicken and dumplings. More than fifty years later, I understand that he really wanted cream and bread. To him it was a delicacy —to her a farm staple.

Several years later, I skimmed the cream off the top of the milk in the glass bottle. We used it on cereal and pudding. It was not thick enough for cream and bread.

In the eye of my mind, I see the glass milk bottles lined neatly on my kitchen step. Frank, the friendly Fairmont milkman, left them Monday, Wednesday and Friday. In addition to milk, he kept us supplied with butter and eggs.

Now waxed and plastic bottles have replaced the glass ones. Milk has become homogeneous. No cream floats to the top. I carry my own milk home from the supermarket.

Berry Picking:
Berry picking genes run in my family. I didn't inherit these genes.

Dad and Grandma were veteran berry pickers. Wild grape, Juneberries, chokecherries and wild plums, Dad knew how and where to find them all.

Mother didn't join the berry pickers. She was allergic to poison ivy. But she made a delightful Juneberry cobbler, jelled the chokecherries and served the tart plum sauce with a dollop of cream.

Rug Beaters:
Our Olson rug needed a spring and fall cleaning. We didn't own a vacuum cleaner so what the carpet sweeper didn't catch, we removed with a rug beater.

Mother and I dragged the nine by twelve rug to the clothesline and somehow, with all our strength, flopped it over two lines.

The rug beater resembled a large metal tennis racket. We beat and swept the dust out of the rug, the dust gritty in our teeth and stuffy in our noses. It was my most unfavorite household task.

It is well to recall some of these memories when I glamorize yesteryear.

THE JUDGMENT

Dr. Hawley stopped Virginia on her way out the door and said, "Virginia, I'm concerned about your essay. Please stop by my office." The young instructor's usual jovial demeanor was changed. There was a scowl between his blue-gray eyes. This was Dr. Hawley's first year of teaching at the small midwestern college. Most students thought he seemed young enough to be one of them.

Virginia stared in disbelief, her heart beating so fast she felt it was visible outside her sweater. Thoughts of her paper tumbled in her mind. *My paper! I worked three weeks on the research and hours more writing more paper. Do you suppose he wants me to publish it? But why the frown? He looked angry.*

She paused for a moment outside the frosted glass of his office door, smoothing her hair with a damp palm, trying to quell her nervousness. Once inside the office she felt more comfortable, almost relaxed.

"Virginia, your term paper appears to be plagiarized. It is so well written that I know you, a college freshman, could not possibly have done it. I'm sure you are aware I'm making a serious charge."

The impact of his message was slow.

Fighting back her tears, she replied, "I most certainly did not plagiarize. My thoughts are my own, my words are my own. When I paraphrase an article, I always give credit to the author."

Angrily, she swung the blue canvas bag from her shoulder and took out the 26 articles that she had used as references to compile her bibliography.

"Dr. Hawley. Before you judge my words, read these articles. I've enjoyed the research and writing my paper on the sex life of a turtle. But I did not plagiarize even one paragraph." Standing tall, her eyes meeting his, she said, "You may contact me when you have looked over the articles."

Holding her head high, Virginia slowly walked through the open door, barely in control of her anger, as the instructor stacked the references on his already cluttered desk without saying a word.

Brushing the tears from her eyes, Virginia tried to gain her composure as she started running down the stairway to her next class. She met her friend, Marge.

"Virginia, Bill has a new friend he wants you to meet. Can you stop by and have pizza with us about seven?"

Marge and Bill were Virginia's closest friends. Happily married, they were notorious for matchmaking.

It will help to divert myself tonight, she thought as she forced a smile from her dry, parched mouth.

"Thanks, Marge. I'd love to meet Bill's friend."

It was difficult to concentrate in her last class and two hours later, when she entered her apartment, the telephone was ringing.

"This is Tom Hawley. Your paper is so unbelievably well written I mistakenly assumed it was plagiarized. I have changed the 'F' to 'A'. Virginia, please forgive me."

Virginia's voice was lilting. "Thank you. I'm so happy you like my writing. That 'A' sounds great!"

"Perhaps, Virginia, I have learned not to make too hasty a judgment. Have a good evening."

As she hung up the phone, Virginia mused, A good evening. Wow, will I ever! I wonder what Bill's friend looks like? What shall I wear?

She danced around in sheer excitement, deciding on a blue sweater to match the blue of her eyes and a short navy blue skirt revealing her shapely legs.

It was a short drive to her friends' home. Composed and lovely, Virginia rang the doorbell.

Bill greeted her at the door. "Virginia, I'd like you to meet Tom Hawley. He's new in town, teaches biology at the college. I've been telling him about you."

A PENNY FOR YOUR THOUGHTS

Some sage told us to save our pennies and the dollars would take care of themselves. Another said, "A penny saved is a penny earned." It has become folklore.

Pennies have a charm about them because they are different from the rest of the coins.

They are larger than a dime and smaller than their cousin, the nickel, and they are copper colored.

Songs such as "Pennies from Heaven" have glorified their copper beauty. Who can imagine a song written about dimes from heaven?

But there is a movement toward eliminating the penny from modern currency. A harsh movement—a ganging up on the little guy.

Imagine a penny so scarce after the year 2150 it would be antique. A penny from 1900, a true copper gemstone, worth its weight in gold.

A cache of copper coins stored in a glass fruit jar or a rusty coffee can found in the attic or basement may put Emily through college in the year 3000.

Those who remember penny candy find it difficult to fathom the lowly penny acquiring antique status.

Many of us have fond memories of great-grandma's collection of pennies housed in a shoebox tied with a shoelace. They provided hours of entertainment. Who hasn't counted pennies with the joy of a Midas?

Newspaper reporters, who currently write of buried treasure at the bottom of the Atlantic, will change to writing of the cache of pennies found in a deserted farm-house. This will spur children to treasure hunt with metal detectors.

Excavation companies will be formed to search through fine sand and black loam for pennies.

Ideas will flourish as to how to store this treasure. Mail order catalogues will be beseiged with orders for penny folders.

In the latter half of the twenty-first century, a movement may arise to reinvent the penny, to give it a place of honor in currency, more honor — more value.

Truly the sage was right, to save our pennies the dollars will take care of themselves — if we wait long enough.

Pennies not legal tender? Science fiction.

CATS AND ME

Long ago I made up my mind not to like cats. Stubbornly, I won't change. All manner of cats have wooed me. Tried their catty wiles on me and purred.

But I have resisted their advances this many years. When I was five I had a best friend kitty. It was a case of unrequited friendship. The more I petted the little white animal, the more she stratched and spit at me. I sat for hours on the barn floor in my blue and white striped coveralls coaxing her to let me hold her. But of no avail.

One day she bolted. Out the double hung barn door, past the watering tank, through the row of weeping willows by the slough into the neighbors' cornfield. I followed but lost her in the rows of corn.

As a lover spurned, that day I made up my mind never, ever to get friendly with a kitty again.

Then a beautiful Persian cat, soft and furry with eyes that melt your heart, entered our family. I reached out a tentative hand to pet her. Before I touched her fur she began to purr in anticipation.

Not even I could resist this warm and friendly addition to our family.

WEAR THAT HAT PROUDLY

"Put on your Easter bonnet . . ." In the ear of my mind I hear the music and in the eye of my mind I see the parade. Hats and beautiful women.

It is interesting how department stores keep featuring hats. But I don't see many women wearing these hats. Time was hats were worn everywhere. Ladies were asked to remove their hats at the movies so others could more easily watch the glamorous stars on the silver screen.

There are few hats in church anymore, only on very young children, dressed in long rosebud print dresses with matching hats. They look lovely, as miniature ladies of another era.

A lady didn't do any serious shopping unless she wore a hat and gloves. Heels, too. A lady always stopped for coffee when shopping. It was an easy excuse to slip out of those heels for a few minutes.

I wish I had saved my hats, at least the most meaningful ones. They would be collector's items.

The first hat I remember wearing was an emerald green velvet with petals framing my face. I loved it as much as a three-year-old can love a confining object like a hat. I cherish the black and white snapshot of the Erickson cousins sitting on the steps of Aunt Helen and Uncle Ole's porch. We little girls are wearing tams or bonnets. I am wearing that emerald green velvet.

The last hat I wore was a red wide-brimmed straw hat with a floppy red flower on its side. It was the only hat in church that Easter Sunday. Embarrassed, I entertained the thought of carrying it in front of me like a giant corsage. Several weeks later, Pastor said, "Some folks perk up their friends by wearing a beautiful red hat." Knowing heads turned to look at me.

Later, I used this hat as an accent piece in my bedroom. My granddaughter loved to parade around the house in it and teeter in my high heels. It became one of my cherished purchases.

An earlier Easter, my aunt gave my cousin and me identical white hats with rolled brims.

I wore a lilac on the left side. Later, I wore it while playing "grownup" with Mother's discarded dresses and shoes. I wish I had saved that hat.

My all-time favorite hat, made of black wool felt, was expensive and flattering. I worried my husband would think it too frivolous. Wearing a black taffeta dress and matching pumps, I proceeded down the stairs. Catching my foot on the second step, my hat flew ahead of me. My husband, helping me to my feet, didn't notice I was wearing a beautiful new hat.

My friend's husband was a pheasant hunter. She covered a hat form with feathers. I wore it proudly with my homemade beige wool suit.

However, Mother was the hat wearer of the family. Each spring and fall she purchased a new hat at Dotty Dunn in Fargo. At Dotty's, a millinery shop, dozens of hats were displayed on tables, shelves and hat forms. There were soft tams of velvet or wool in black, brown, navy or red; helmet-like felt cloches with narrow brims; picture hats in white, lavender, yellow and pink, their floppy brims trimmed with contrasting bows and flowers. There were hats crowned high with feathers or fur. Dotty Dunn's was a hat wearer's paradise.

Mother was greeted at the door by a smiling milliner and seated on a stool in front of a small kidney-shaped table backed by an oversized mirror. After Mother stated her preference for shape and color, the milliner returned with five to eight hats. She carefully positioned each hat, then handed Mother a mirror so she could see the back. Mother always found just the perfect hat.

From a nearby stool, I watched for a long time, until I retreated into my imagination. I imagined Blondie, of the Sunday comics, walking into the shop on high stiletto heels. She was, in my imagination, even more beautiful than depicted in the paper. Dagwood Bumstad visited with my father on a bench near the front door until he had to carry out all the hatboxes. For Blondie, unlike Mother, wasn't satisfied with one lovely new hat.

Mother loved veils. When summer humidity caused them to go limp, she added body by ironing them with wax paper. One of her hats was crowned with so many feathers it looked like a bird was perched on her head ready to take flight. Her picture, in black and white, doesn't do it justice. Years later, I was to remember that hat when a bird flew into the sanctuary during services. It was nearly as distracting as her hat.

Walking by those fantastic hat displays in the department stores evokes all these memories. I plan to go shopping and buy one of those beautiful hats to wear proudly on Easter Sunday. Just for the sake of old times.

Dearest Mom,

It's the first time I've written a letter to anyone and addressed it to heaven. I may not have a prayer of a chance at priority mail and your zip code is most elusive but I thought I'd give it a try.

I'm writing this while seated at the old oak library table, the one at which you taught me to read and write before I started to school. As Pastor Mark said at your memorial service, teaching was your passion.

Today I miss you with that choked up, full-throat feeling for it will be the first time I have given a reading without rehearsing it with you.

I can hear you say, "Slow down, speak more slowly, that's good vocal expression and eye contact but don't forget the pause." I know that both of us were amused but also valued your speech instructions.

Mother, I miss you. You who launched my balloon over a half century ago, you who were my life-long drama coach and faithful cheerleader, you, my very best friend. Please give my love to God.   Eternally yours,

Angela

TALES OF SHOE LEATHER

S-H-O-E was the first word I spelled. It was printed in black on an orange sign hung in front of the village shoe store. Not quite three, I loved shoes. It was a love affair which was to last the next half century and more.

How pleased that little girl would be if she could look inside my closet and see all the shoes. Some with strange heels are more than twenty years old. But what a spectacular collection of black, brown, gray, white and red shoes made of suede, cowhide, fabric and plastic.

My first hard soled shoe holds paper clips on my desk, it is a dull cracked patent leather with brown shoelaces. I expect the brown laces once were white. It is strange that there is only one shoe because I had two active feet. Mother said I never walked, I ran and hadn't stopped running.

Now I proudly wear my very first boots. They are hand-tooled beauties with neatly concealed zippers at the back of the heel. I am thankful for those zippers for it would be impossible to ease my foot through the narrow top of the boot. The boots, as most of my shoes, were an impulse purchase. I wore them out of the store confident every woman I met was looking covetously at my boot clad feet.

I wore navy blue sandals at my first wedding. They were comfortable and practical. I wore them for the next fifteen years until I wore a hole in the sole.

When Bill and I were married, I wore pumps with

alligator trim. They were so uncomfortable I removed them during the reception and greeted guests in my stocking feet. I wear them occasionally if I know I'll be seated at least 7/8 of the time. My glamorous aunt from Chicago visited us when I was eight years old. She forgot her diminutive black patent pumps. I had never seen anything so beautiful for Mother encased her tiny narrow foot in black orthopedic horrors. My aunt's shoes fit me perfectly and, tottering in the three-inch heels, I imagined I was Princess Elizabeth of England who was twenty days older than I.

I carefully draped a discarded blue brocaded drape on a highchair for my throne. Not much business of state was conducted because I was too busy admiring my feet. Within a week the shoes were mailed to their rightful owner and it was to be more than a decade before I would again wear a patent leather pump.

I walked two miles to a one-room country school wearing black or brown oxfords. I had two pairs of shoes, one for school, the other one for church. My school shoes became dusty as did my anklets and feet. The foot perspiration and dirt inside the shoe made a nasty sludge. Evenings, I scraped out the sludge onto a newspaper. Always the shoes were more comfortable and roomy when I wore them the next day. My Sunday shoes eventually became my school shoes and I would sport a new pair on Sunday morning.

In high school I graduated to two pair of shoes for school and one for special events. Black and white saddles with colorful plaid laces were popular. I never polished those saddle shoes because the crowd, to which I aspired, always wore dirty saddles.

Haraches, shoes resembling flat brown baskets, were the shoes of the day. They had slippery leather soles and, as spirited horses, they were hard to control. I fell at least three embarrassing times on the polished maple floors of the study hall.

For forty years I wore a white nurse's oxford, always a planned utilitarian purchase. I polished them diligently with an opaque white liquid. The same polish I now use for my white leather golf shoes.

My favorite shoes are my newest shoes. They are black suede pumps with a heel curving as a bell at the bottom. They resemble the shoes mother wore when a young woman, years before she started wearing those orthopedic horrors.

Although I adore shoes, I remove them when I enter the house and collect a variety at the front and back doors. Eventually I carry them to the closet where they lie sprawled on the floor.

Soon I will fastidiously sort my shoes by color and check them for repair. I may even find a shoe treasure lying under the closet rubble.

NOT JUST A HOUSE

We lived in the kitchen of the farm home where I
spent my childhood. This kitchen, as most farm
kitchens, was dominated by a wood range; the oven
catch was broken and a small piece of charred wood
held the oven door shut.

My favorite spot was the black-tin woodbox. In the
winter it was filled with crisp snow covered split wood
soon to sizzle and crackle in the fire. Empty in the summer, it became a car, a pirate ship or a hiding place.
Balancing my sturdy brown shoes on its lid, I recited
poetry to my fantasy friends until Mother complained,
"Angela, you make more noise than a dozen."

Mother loved green. Our kitchen windows were
clocked in green dotted swiss and the table was covered
with a green checked oilcloth. Red geraniums in green
crepe paper covered coffee cans stood on the window
sills. The kitchen sink drained outside in the summer and
indoors to a pail in the winter. A pail with a dipper stood
next to the sink on a green oilcloth covered shelf.

The living room, Mother's friends said, was cozy.
There was no upholstered furniture, only a cot which
opened with effort to a double bed.

A built-in book shelf housed Dad's Zane Grey nov-
els and Mother's large black encyclopedias. The bottom
shelf, I discovered, was easily removed to reveal a secret
hiding place for my diary and a special Valentine.

The home I lived in the longest had three bedrooms,

all upstairs. One I shared with my husband and the other two were occupied by four boys. Downstairs the living room featured a unique birch fireplace. Nothing in that living room matched. The new chair waited years for the new sofa. By that time the chair would be faded and worn. The bay window in the dining room was full of plants. If there was illness or a family crisis the plants weren't watered. They, as I, got tired and droopy.

These houses have provided a sanctuary from the world. Each one, in turn, my home.

THE GENTLE GIANT

Your youngest son comes to visit. The gentle giant. Over a foot taller than you, he lifts you from the floor in a bear hug.

You remember the day he was born. He didn't fit the dress or bonnet any better than his three older brothers. The blue romper barely fit. After his birth you gave away the little white dress. You almost forgot you wanted a girl, he was such a handsome hunk of boy baby.

You remember your hoarseness yelling at high school regional and state wrestling matches.

Wrestling, a microcosm of life.

You look forward to his visit. His humor. His hugs.

IRRITATIONS, GREAT AND SMALL

The major irritations I can handle. Just fine. It's the minor irritations which plummet me to despair.

Most minor irritations are with my friends—or heaven forbid—my family. It all started with my mom.

"You must always wear bangs, dear, your forehead is so high."

My bangs floated with the prairie winds. All my life I struggled with those bangs until last year, in a celebration of life, I let my bangs grow. My hair grows five and one eighth inches a year so the growing out process was painstaking. My high rounded forehead is now exposed, no bang worries but what would Mom think of the grand expose?

I miss one of my minor irritants. I'd run to the phone knowing it was Mother when it stopped after the third ring. I wish I could hear those three rings but technology isn't advanced enough for her to call from heaven. I also miss her correcting my grammar. I expect God has appointed her heaven's grammarian.

I dress for a party and find the other guests are casually attired. I dress casually for the next party and find the other guests are wearing designer gowns.

A Christmas ornament I've cherished for more than fifty years shatters on the living room rug.

I lean to pick it up and I grimace from that low back pain I've noticed for the last twenty years.

A friend carelessly comments, "You look so nice today."

That word, today, echoes and achieves a life of its own. How did she think I looked yesterday? Tacky? Apparently not nice. Nice is such a dowdy word. Ordinary.

Elegant, a state-of-the-art word, would have been better. Or the friend could lie and say, "You look beautiful, as always." Even "You always look so nice," would be better, far better.

Another friend tells me I'm too busy and then proceeds to tell me that if I were as busy as she, I wouldn't have time to sing in the choir or to join in the ladies' golf league. Then I feel lazy.

Most minor irritations happen when I have guests. The meringue on my lemon pie is watery and flat. I shatter a glass on the kitchen floor before I answer the doorbell. As the guest enters, I spy a cobweb near the front door. I imagine a cricket chirping in the laundry room.

Later, when Bill is asking a blessing at dinner, we're interrupted by a telemarketing phone call.

"Thank you for calling," I tell her, "I don't need my carpet cleaned."

I've decided to dispense with petty irritations by changing them to major irritations, thus eliminating them. The next time a friend says, "You look nice today," I'll say, "Thank you, I think I looked great yesterday, too."

I'll hang up the telephone on the telemarketer. I'll learn to tolerate an occasional spider web. I may even cut those bangs again. I miss them. Mother did know best.

A SON REMEMBERED

The tiny pink ruffled dress didn't fit this all boy body. The blue romper I had taken to the hospital, just in case there was to be a third boy, fit snuggly over his beautiful little body.

Hours after contracting measles at eleven months, Douglas was hospitalized in critical condition with labored respirations. He was placed in an oxygen tent and given antibiotics for

ten days. The residuals of what was thought in 1955 to be a simple childhood disease left Doug changed.

Testing a few I.Q. points too high for special education classes he struggled, labeled a slow learner, in the classroom. He compensated with a delightful sense of humor, coining names for his friends and family. One of his friends was a girl with Down's Syndrome whom he taught with infinite patience to ride a tricycle.

One of the girls in his class said, "Doug may not be the smartest but he is the nicest boy in our class."

Always adept with his hands, he built elaborate creations from his erector set and enjoyed battery operated toys. It was no surprise to me to receive a small battery charger for my birthday. After opening the package, I never saw his gift again.

One of his brothers was frustrated with a less than perfect spelling paper. Doug consoled him with "Think nothing of it, sometimes I get only one right."

Puberty changed things. At age thirteen, Doug was overcome with feelings of inadequacy and failure. His blue eyes looked forlorn and his speech was slowed.

He sat on the floor in a fetal position crying with heart-breaking sobs, stuffing kleenex in his mouth and nose.

The labels varied from social worker to psychologist to neurologist: slow learner, retarded, school phobia, schizophrenia and finally, manic depression.

Also called bipolar disorder, manic depression is a major mental illness characterized by alternating extremely high and low moods without relevance to circumstances. Doug was more often depressed than manic. He was admitted to the hospital and placed on antidepressant therapy.

After a year of three hospitalizations interposed with homebound tutoring, Doug was transferred to the adolescent unit of the state hospital. During the fifty mile trip, he consoled his father and me.

"Don't look so sad, Dad. Don't cry, Mother. I'll be all right."

Arriving home, I repeated a litany of frustration, "Why, God, why?" a prayer born of fatigue as I pondered the events of the day. A day which was to be forever etched in my memory. The events of this longest day caved in on me much as a broken down mattress fails to support a tired body, its coils, as my brain, stressed from years of tension.

I prepared chili that evening for my husband and three other sons. Cutting my finger on the can of tomatoes and applying a bandage to my finger, I wished it would be as simple to fix Doug's depression. A band-aid approach. I smiled wryly at the thought. The door burst open with my youngest son.

"Mom, what happened to Doug?" We cried together.

Our family couldn't visit Doug for three weeks. He made a good adjustment to the hospital and planned to bring his dog, Tiny, to live with him. After one patient put his pet cat in the washer, the rules changed and no pets were allowed.

Patients were given time out in an isolation room with padded walls for rule infractions. Doug was in the room frequently for his compulsion to pat people on their head. It never changed his behavior.

After the first year in the hospital Doug came home on weekends. His brothers and friends met him at the train depot. He spent most of the weekends in our garage working on his bike repair business, always with a circle of friends watching him work. I enjoyed the laughter in the garage when I served them lemonade and cookies.

Doug was busy as the owner of the local ice cream shop encouraged him to put a sign in the window which read, "Bikicile repair" with his phone number. In spite of the spelling, the bikes always worked. He charged a nickel or a dime, even a quarter if it was a big job.

Doug attended a one-room school on the state hospital campus. A kindhearted teacher praised any progress and in this nonthreatening atmosphere he made substantial remedial progress.

After three years in the hospital, Doug was discharged at sixteen years of age. We had a wonderful family celebration and life assumed a degree of normalcy for all of us.

That fall he enrolled in a carpentry class at the vocational school. He took pride in his first basic project, a wooden tray for his tools.

Doug attended the vocational school Halloween

dance. I went to bed secure that he would return soon after the dance for just the week before he had assured me, "You know, Mom, I always like to come home."

At six in the morning we were awakened by the doorbell. There were three people, my friend, her husband and their priest.

"There has been an accident."

"Who is dead?" I said, thinking it must be our son, a freshman in an out-of-state college.

We then heard the impossible. Doug was dead. As a pedestrian, he was struck by a car and killed. Life was to be never the same for our family.

In grief, my abdominal muscles contracted as in labor. When Doug was born they became more intense and frequent. As he entered into eternal life, the contractions were less intense and further apart.

The next few days over one hundred fifty friends, relatives and acquaintances stopped by our home. Their loving arms upheld us.

The bronze casket was wheeled slowly out of the full church into the sunny November afternoon. I placed my hand on its lid and felt the reassurance that, in the Christian view of eternal life, death at sixteen or sixty is irrelevant.

Two days after Doug's death, our pastor and I visited his grave on which I placed a huge bouquet of garden flowers. Flowers which Doug and I had planted that spring.

A PERFECT WEDDING

The scent of flowers fills the air. More than thirty faces ripple with affection as the bride and groom walk into the church lounge.

The bride is beautiful, her honey-colored hair crowned by a wreath of daisies is loose on her shoulders.

Their attendants, her sister and his friend, flank the couple as the mother of the bride and her soon-to-become son-in-law sing a song of love and faith.

The pastor starts, "We are gathered together in the presence of God . . ."

In his opening remarks, he credits the many Bible verses he uses as selected by the bride and groom for their wedding.

He explains in his sermon that God took the rib of Adam for a reason, rather than a rib from his head, so Adam wouldn't lord it over his wife; rather than a bone from his feet so he would not tower over her, he chose a rib from the center of his being to show they were equal, walking side by side throughout life.

Tenderly they exchanged rings.

"As God has joined together, let no man put asunder."

Thus, this happy couple started their new life together with the blessings of God, family and friends.

TEARS AND MORE TEARS

"Why are you crying, Mommie?"Four-year-old Sara's question only made Jane cry harder.

Picking her up and cradling her in her arms, she answered, "Honey, Mommie loves you so much and I'm worried about you. You have been sick a long time so I talked with Dr. Pearson."

Sara nestled closer to her mother. Fair of skin with blonde hair and blue eyes, Sara was a beautiful child. Now her skin pale, she complained frequently of headaches and had lost her appetite. She also had a recurrent high temperature. They had an appointment with Dr. Pearson the next day.

After a careful examination, during which he questioned Jane about Sara's symptoms, he said, "To rule out acute lymphobastic leukemia, I'm ordering a biopsy of lymph nodes, bloodwork and a bone marrow test."

Frightened, Jane had difficulty hearing what Dr. Pearson said after that dreaded word, leukemia. Jane, waiting anxiously for the test to be completed, worried Sara would be frightened by the long biopsy needles but consoled herself that Sara trusted Dr. Pearson.

The next morning Sara ate half of her breakfast and was more interested in her toys.

The phone rang at 10:30 a.m.

"Dr. Pearson? Oh, thank you, what wonderful news."

Overjoyed that the tests were negative, Jane started crying as she hung up the phone. Sara, rocking her baby doll, looked up.

"Mommie, why are you crying?"

OF PICTURES
AND GRANDCHILDREN

Bill and I have handsome grandchildren. With our combined families, we have an even dozen. I decided to frame a picture of each of them and scatter the photos around the living room. The problem is we have received new pictures in different sizes and we have to make decisions whether to frame the new or leave the old.

If we frame a second picture of each, we could end up with twenty-four pictures. This, in time, could pyramid as a chain letter, spilling from the table and piano to the desk and floor.

I look at these beautiful children lovingly each day until I almost forget which are my grandchildren and which are Bil's. I only know that they are ours and I am grateful.

THE EMPTY NEST

A wren builds his nest
in my blue ceramic birdhouse.
His head out the little
round door of his home,
he advertises for a mate.
He flies high to the roof
and continues his frantic call.
He hops to a tree branch
and becomes both visible and vocal,
but to no avail.
His nest stands empty,
the twigs askew.
His mating call ignored,
no eggs in his nest.

A PINK SILK STRING

Recently I found an old faded pink necktie knitted by my grandmother one hundred and twenty years ago.

Grandma was remarkable in her insight, a truly discerning woman. Each of her ten grand-children felt he or she was her favorite. Except for my sister, her namesake, who flushed an apple core down Grandma's toilet. We plunged to no avail and Grandma resorted to phoning the plumber. It was a catastrophic event.

Woe to any other than the ten of us if they called her "Grandma."

"I am not a grandma to every Tom, Dick and Harry," she said.

A study in contrasts, this grandma of mine, quick of wit and hand, warm and sarcastic, feisty to the embarrassment of her family. She was gentle, yet sharp of tongue, with a gift of mimicry.

Every day, except Sunday when she did no work, Grandma, at age sixty-five, baked four apple, three pump-

kin and three lemon pies in addition to five dozen dough-
nuts, for a restaurant.

She made an additional pie a week, usually apple,
for herself. Her baking was ready and her kitchen clean
by seven in the morning.

I visited her often while in high school and nursing
school, not only for a piece of wonderful pie, but she loaned
me money which I repaid promptly to keep my credit good.

Grandma emigrated from Norway at the age of eighteen. She worked as a nanny for a Chicago family for
four years. During this time she became proficient at
reading and writing English.

She joined other relatives in Minnesota and opened
a dressmaker shop. An excellent seamstress, the wealth-
iest ladies in town wore her creations proudly.

Once a beautiful young girl, delicate of frame with
good legs, trim ankles and tiny feet, arthritis had brought
its burdens. Her small frame was crunched by the crip-
pling disease. One day she limped to the crowded buffet in her dining room and found a string-like faded pink
necktie and told me this story.

"I had two boyfriends, both wanted to marry me. I
couldn't decide because both were good men. One rich,
with a large farm. The other, poor, but had gentle quiet
ways. I knit this pink silk necktie thinking I would give
it to the one I would marry. I put the necktie in my
pocket when I went for a buggy ride with the wealthy
man. I knew I could not marry him and I told him so.

"The next evening I went for a walk with the man
who became your grandpa. I knew he would be a
good father for my children so I told him I'd marry him
and I gave him the necktie. Angela, I want you to have
this necktie."

Years later, I told Mother this story.

"So that is why it was Dad's favorite necktie. He had
several but always wore the homemade pink one."

BUT I CAME BACK

You ask about your grandson. "He moved out of the house today." Tears cascade your cheeks. You hope your son doesn't hear the tremor in your voice.

"It was a worst day of my life kind of day when you left home."

"But I came back."

You sit by the phone for a very long time after this conversation. You recall your brave smile, your wit, your courage when he, also college bound, left home.

You extrapolate a memory from its bank . . . the day that he, your eldest son, is born. When you mentally race out of the building, down four flights of red linoleum covered stairs to the front door of the hospital. You imagine sitting on the slivered oak bench between the two elm trees in front of this hospital named for the healer, St. Luke. Looking at the October leaves swirling around your feet, you think — this is only a tumor.

Your racing mind returns to foggy reality with those miracle words, "It's a boy."

Your maternal fingers touch his blood tinged hair and his petal soft cheeks. You, as all mothers, count fingers and toes.

In your reverie you feel again, as if for the first time, the delight of his first step, his first word, his joyous laugh.

You remember dressing him in stiff new jeans and a blue and white striped short-sleeved shirt, short days before his sixth birthday, his blonde hair slicked off his forehead. You walk with him the three blocks to his school, his hand moist in yours.

His teacher is friendly and has a reputation for competence. Her smile reassures you.

You walk home with your neighbor. Neither of you talk. The lump in your throat is too big, you suspect hers is too.

Eight eternal hours later, you hear, "I'm home, Mama."

Your mind fast forwards to his high school graduation. You think, as he marches to "Pomp and Circumstance," that he is the most handsome boy in his class.

After a year of college, he volunteers for Viet Nam. You wonder if and when he will come home. Your cheerfulness doesn't fool him. Neither you nor he are letter writers but for a very long time part of yourself is missing.

And he comes back.

And returns to college with renewed determination.

He marries. This girl who becomes the mother of your first born grandson.

Your grandson resembles your son—same smile, same humor. At three he draws a picture of the flames in the fireplace and you know he is an artist.

Three years later your first granddaughter arrives. She of the lively presence from the day of birth, charms you. Her latest photograph, on the piano, smiles at you.

Your joints remind you that you are no longer young and that you have been sitting nearly two hours by the telephone.

During those two hours, in the eye of your mind, you have seen your son come full circle and in the ear of your mind, you have heard him say, "But I came back."

PSALM 121   A SONG OF PRAISE

I will lift up my eyes unto the hills from whence cometh my help.

A large hill looms skyward, a half-mile from my home. Climbing until I reach the summit, I sit on a large granite rock and look over the top of boxelder and oak trees to see the steeple of Rollag Church where I will be confirmed in early October.

I stand on this rock and recite the 121st Psalm. I hear a meadowlark and a crow in the distance. I think about God's plan for my life.

My help cometh from the Lord which made heaven and earth.

At age fourteen, I don't realize this same Psalm will comfort me the rest of my life. It will help me rear four sons, each with their own thoughts and dreams.

He will not suffer thy foot to be moved; He that keepeth thee will not slumber.

At the bedside of a sick child, He is with me. During the mental illness of another, He comforts me.

Behold He that keeps Israel shall neither slumber or sleep.

During the death of my child, He does not slumber or sleep.

The Lord is thy Keeper, the Lord is thy shade upon they right hand.

My husband is comforted on his death bed. The Lord is the shade on his right hand.

The Lord shall preserve thee from all evil; He shall preserve thy soul.

The 121st Psalm is woven into the wedding sermon during the 62nd year of my life.

The Lord shall preserve thy going out and thy coming in from this time forth and even forevermore.

From childhood to middle age and now golden age, I continue to be sheltered by the words of this Song of Praise.